TheRhythmEffect

The Leader's Guide to Team Performance

It's not how hard you work,
it's how well you synchronise

PAULFARINA

This book is published by FES Publishing.

ISBN 978-0-6489447-0-6

Printed in Australia.

Cover design, internal design and copy-editing:
Lauren Shay – Full Stop Writing, Editing and Design.

For my parents, Bert and Fran.

Your words over the years were not wasted; I hear them every day,
and I am grateful to no end.

"Being a leader is a journey, not a destination. We are continually learning, reflecting and refining as we go. In working with Paul, the key message was to STOP, take some time to reflect and consider is there a better way to manage, is there a better way to achieve results.

"The Rhythm Effect is a journey through reflection and a reminder that we are all learning how to manage, how to let go, how to build trust and how to view the world from a different perspective. A refreshing approach to management and leadership."
– Brett Connell, CEO of Victorian Amateur Football Association

"The Rhythm Effect is a fresh and unique approach to leading high-performing cultures. Paul has been able to collate and craft easy-to-use frameworks for high achievers wanting to be the best leader they can be. Modern-day leaders are under tremendous pressure, leading to more hours and more resources being used up to gain results. Paul proposes an alternative that is both inspirational and practical for leaders of all personality types. The utilisation of rhythm as a performance concept is an exciting prospect in our contemporary business environment."
– Dominique Lamb, Chief Executive Officer, National Retail Association

"Paul has a rare depth of quality thinking around how to get the most return from our effort. In a world where leaders of teams are under more pressure than ever to leverage their knowledge, skills and often limited resources, *The Rhythm Effect* will help to accelerate the progress and fulfillment of not only the workplace, but the community."
– Christina Guidotti, CEO of Leading Women

"The Rhythm Effect just makes sense. Let the universal laws of physics work in your favour, subtly apply them to your leadership and watch your results seemingly become easier to obtain … as when you're in rhythm, life conspires with you!

"Paul's book saves the modern leader hours and hours of reading the best business and leadership books. It's a go-to manual for inspiration. He succinctly distils the key concepts of the great leadership authors whilst using real-life stories and examples you can connect with … regularly nodding your head, thinking, 'That's me!' Get your rhythm on!"
– Alex Ouwens, Managing Director, Ouwens Casserly Real Estate

"*The Rhythm Effect* lays bare the expectation on leaders, workers and teams that are driven to achieve greater productivity (more for less) in working environments with limited resources. Pressure, anxiety and sheer exhaustion are common by-products of meeting challenging targets (that keep on coming)! For leaders and teams in this trap, the impacts are profound on family, social and recreational lives. There has to be a better way to strive for high performance without burning out.

"This book uses the author's life experiences in professional sport and corporate environments, research outcomes and sage advice from successful leaders to illustrate the problem. The solution – called the Rhythm Effect – provides a pragmatic approach for leaders and teams to work within a holistic framework to achieve rhythm and, ultimately, high-performing teams."

– Tony McDonald, Project Director, ANZ Bank

"*The Rhythm Effect* is a unique approach to leading high-performing cultures. The frameworks allow practical implementation for leaders to be their best in establishing an environment where team members can be winners. Leaders are under tremendous pressure to deliver results, many making the mistake of throwing more hours and more resources to deliver them. Paul proposes an alternative that is both inspirational and pragmatic for leaders of all backgrounds and experience levels. The utilisation of rhythm as a performance concept is an exciting prospect in our contemporary business environment."

– Dan Collins, Olympic medallist and world champion, speaker, mentor and performance coach

"At the time of reading *The Rhythm Effect*, the world was still trying to make sense of the social and economic impact of COVID-19. Leaders find themselves looking around the corner at ways to continue maximising their productivity and performance, with a greater appetite for working smarter, not harder.

"Paul provides a pathway for leaders to access this performance concept and presents to the reader in a way that makes it practical and easy to apply. A must-read for anyone curious about achieving greatness as a leader, effortlessly."

– Jaquie Scammell, Australia's leading customer service expert and author, Service Mindset and Service Habits

"*The Rhythm Effect* provides established and developing leaders with a comprehensive framework based on the power of rhythm to enable the development of successful businesses built on positive culture and high-performing, motivated independent teams."

– David Cruttenden, Senior Media and Broadcast Consultant, Former ABC Director of Resources

"We've all seen them; most of us have felt their wrath. The proponents of the 'try harder' mindset, with just the one trick in their kitbag: seeking to exhort greater effort from already exhausted bodies and minds. This mindset has been carried from generation to generation, coach to coach, leader to leader. Many of us have become them.

"But in my experience, 30 years in elite sport, nothing good happens when people are pushed to exhaustion. Fun is replaced by fear. Yes, effort is required, but it is only a ticket to the game. I also learned that sport is not team versus team or club versus club. It is system versus system. We need a better system to elicit higher performance.

"In your hand is the system. It is built on lived experience. The best of business. The best of sport. Immediately accessible and applicable. It is a leader's leadership tool kit. Paul Farina's *The Rhythm Effect* is the system you and your team needs to build teams and organisations based on insight and understanding – the stuff that matters. And that's when the fun starts."

– Cameron Schwab, CEO and founder, designCEO

"Rethinking and re-imagining not just what we do but how we do it is key to maintaining and improving individual, team and company performance. On top of this, modern-day leaders are under tremendous pressure, resulting in longer hours and more resources being used up to gain results.

"In his latest book, Paul Farina shares a fresh and unique approach to leading high-performing cultures. Using personal story, insight and research, Paul has been able to collate and craft easy-to-use frameworks for high achievers wanting to be the best leader they can be. Paul proposes an alternative that is both inspirational and practical for leaders of all personality types. This book is perfect for anyone who wants to improve performance in the new business world."

– Janine Garner, keynote speaker, bestselling author, mentor, Director, Curious Minds AUS Pty Ltd

Contents

About This Book

This book is a refined body of work for quick and easy access with one goal in mind:

To take conceptual and theoretical ideas of high performance and present them in a practical, tangible framework for professional leaders.

Colleagues and mentors have described me as a "complex thinker". This is not always a compliment. It refers to my natural tendency to overthink and complicate matters by deeply considering all details, some of which may not be relevant. I also naturally take a philosophical and conceptual approach to problem solving, which serves me well in some scenarios but creates friction in others.

When I played cricket as an overseas professional in the UK, my way of thinking caused me great frustration. It created endless distractions and aggravations, so I did what I knew best: I bit my lip and threw pure hard work at it.

I trained harder. In a game situation, I would force my performance through brutal strong will. This created some good results, but it came at a cost. A lot of the time, my cricket performance suffered and created a negative spiral of self-doubt and mental fragility. I suffered physically, leaving all sorts of problems for an array of chiropractors, physiotherapists and massage therapists to solve. I also worked beyond my body's energy capacity, creating energy deficits that left me with long-term fatigue issues, making recovery a full-time job.

No matter what your vocation is, forcing a result is required sometimes. But when it becomes our daily default, we can find ourselves in a dark and fragile place.

When I climbed the corporate ladder after my sporting career finished, I found the same patterns of thinking and behaviour forming. The strong work ethic my parents instilled in me was the main tool I reached for in my toolbox – particularly when I was in a new job or working on a new project.

Then, as a manager, not only was I working harder and longer hours to get my results, I was also cleaning up after my team. Do you remember the old cliché, *"If you want to do a job properly, do it yourself"*? Yes, I said this to myself a lot. I constantly filled in the cracks left by my team. If a customer was not followed up, I would make the call. If there were dirty dishes in the staffroom sink, I would clean them. If reports were not filled in properly … you get the idea. While doing all this, I would grit my teeth – not because it was difficult, but because it annoyed the hell out of me! And it wasn't fun.

After consulting business clients for more than a decade, it is my observation that these nightmarish working patterns are widespread. It's not just me! My business-owning clients seem to prescribe to the same mantras. The issues of working harder, longer and trying to do it all yourself affect many professionals and people in leadership roles.

My observations have brought me to the following conclusions:

- It is not a profitable way of working.
- It is not a fun way of working.
- But it is a comfortable way of working.

Something I haven't told you yet is that I have a natural disposition towards being a couch potato. Yes, even though I built a reputation for keeping my head down and working through the problems in front of me, the only thing I really wanted to do was relax. Chill out. Kick it back into second gear. Don't we all?! It was because of this that I could never understand why people worked 60, 70 or 80 hours a week, then wore this like a badge of honour. I always thought it was such an uninteresting way to spend one's waking hours. There is so much more to life than work, isn't there?

I also felt that working these long hours was a signal of incompetence (on one level or another). I know this sounds harsh, but I believe many of us could do each other's jobs, given the right environmental factors. You are reading this book right now, but I know you could write your own book on leading teams (if you haven't already). I was a sales manager, and I believe almost anyone could be a sales manager if they wanted to. If this is true, then the game we play at work is not one of achieving a set outcome; it is a game of doing the job in the allotted time (i.e. a typical working week), within the allocated resource expenditure, and replicating this on an ongoing basis in the face of challenges that are out of our control.

But how do we do it? What is the secret sauce? And how do we apply the secret sauce to our individual situations?

It is my belief that we can work in a calm, considered and caring way that yields infinite results. When I look at the times I was flying and killing it (or "crushing it", as Gary Vaynerchuk would say), I was at my most relaxed. I wasn't overthinking or forcing anything. I wasn't even working very hard. It was as if I wasn't even there.

Sportspeople refer to these moments as "being in the zone". Times when it all clicks; when great work gets produced easily and without much effort, and things just happen (in a good way).

My work focuses on how we can access these moments, extend them, and make them repeatable and accessible for team members, leaders, and entire organisations. I call this *rhythm*.

The principles of rhythm come together to create *the Rhythm Effect*. Like a ripple effect, where there is amplification beyond ourselves and those we interact with to create powerful influence, the Rhythm Effect is when acceleration, meaningful progress and infinite ripples are felt within a community. No matter where your starting point is, it's a way of working that enables you to increase your Return On Effort (ROE) and achieve unimaginable outcomes with low to no expenditure.

Before you get stuck in, a word on how to utilise the ideas in this book. I will take you through the macro frameworks of rhythm. It is a large undertaking, and for some, it may feel overwhelming. To ensure the content is accessible, here are some key considerations for any leader who wants to bring more rhythm into their leadership and the workflows of their team:

1. All ingredients discussed in this book are a great starting point. Many are actionable immediately, but the starting point for you will probably be different from your counterpart in another department.

2. Prioritise the small actions. These are things you can do straight away and may include: finding out information to reduce blank spots in an area, talking with a team member using one of the tools, or writing down some thoughts to make sense of things as they stand. Many small actions compound to form impactful change; so, leverage this rather than put heavy expectations on yourself.

3. I work with leaders and organisations of all types, helping them decipher the Rhythm Effect and the many moving parts of building synchronisation into their workplace cultures. This book is a starting point for discovering this deep and powerful concept. I run full-day, online and multi-day training programs on the subjects covered in this book. I work one-on-one with managers, providing mentoring programs, as well as coaching programs for executives. I also speak at conferences to spread the word of rhythm and write for various association and trade publications. More information can be found at www.paulfarina.com.au.

4. Rhythm is a performance topic. All individuals can leverage rhythm, and every individual can be a leader. This book is written specifically for leaders of teams to help them to understand the principles of rhythm. The first half of the book introduces the concepts of rhythm, so leaders can diagnose their own leadership rhythm and plot their teams' current rhythm abilities. The second half discusses the ways rhythm can be built.

5. Building rhythm and leading with rhythm is an incremental game. Prioritising the areas of this book that relate the most to your workplace is a great way to access rhythm. Building actions on top of each other and "drilling them in" over time is a clever way for leaders to slowly but surely create drastic cultural change.

I hope you enjoy exploring rhythm as much as I have enjoyed researching and collating these frameworks. This is merely the tip of the iceberg of such an important and useful subject. It's exciting, and I invite you to join me to instil these ideas in your team, organisation and community. Who knows where they can take us?

Play well.
Paul

Join the Community

As you will read, friction can be a serious problem in our workplaces!

Throughout this book, I refer to resources, models and ways of working that can help you and your team increase workflow effectiveness and overcome the constant forces trying to knock you out of rhythm.

More resources to watch, read and download are available at:

www.paulfarina.com.au/resources

This book represents an opportunity to join others looking to create positive outcomes without "killing themselves" in the process (or those around them!). As you read through the book, I invite you to make notes, experiment with ideas, and join the discussion around high-performing environments and cultures that pierce the hectic busyness of modern life.

Check out The Boot Room. This is where a great crew of professionals from around the world enjoy extra resources, insights, my latest research and other helpful stuff:

www.paulfarina.com.au/home/#the-boot-room

And if you are a part of a book club, you can download discussion questions, ideas for reflection and other resources at www.paulfarina. com.au/resources.

Introduction

Hard Work (The Old Paradigm)

I was born to Italian immigrants who came to Australia in the 1950s. It was the aftermath of World War II. Europe was a bit of a mess, and many Europeans made the big boat trip to various countries of opportunity. Places like Australia, Canada and the USA all welcomed people into their country. However, there were many integration issues, which we still feel and see to this day.

These immigrants brought with them their culture, their wonderful food and rituals, which help make up our modern communities. And, generally, the one thing they did more than anyone else was work hard. They worked their butts off! Working hard was the only resource they had, other than each other. They were poor and it was a matter of survival. Many did well. They created a life for themselves, took care of their families, and created opportunities for the next generation.

In Adelaide, where I was born, the Italians formed a reputation for being the best builders in town. When it came to construction, they did it, and they did it well. My father, Umberto (Bert), worked on a building site for his older brother, attending trade school at night to get his carpentry qualification. He then worked incredibly hard to get his builder's license and, finally, built his own business, Bert Farina Constructions Pty Ltd.

Of course, it wasn't just Dad who worked hard. Mum, Frances (Fran), was right there with him. Not only did she raise us kids, but she also administered every document that went through the home-based office. I still remember half waking to the thuds of the old-school typewriter as

Mum pounded away in the early hours of the morning. She then served us all breakfast at 7am and got us off to school each day with clean clothes and a packed lunch.

I look back at those days and wonder how they did it. It was with a great work ethic and a lot of sacrifices. This ethos has been instilled in many of us by our parents, teachers and bosses. If in doubt, work hard. Still in doubt? Work even harder.

This way of thinking has some merit. If you don't work hard, you will never master anything or get anywhere in life. But in this modern age, I feel the term "work hard" has lost some of its meaning. And I wonder if it really is the answer in the first place.

My parents were successful, but the long work hours, stress and strain caused them many health problems, especially for my father. It's so easy to cocoon ourselves in our work and isolate ourselves from our peers, subordinates and families. We can become judgmental of others and approach situations with a closed mind. And when hard work doesn't get the job done, what options do we have left?

Further to this, I think the idea of working harder can leave us feeling lost. How do you work harder when you are already trying as hard as you can? How do you work harder when you are already putting down unpaid overtime, which you know you'll never get back in lieu? How do you work harder when you are already giving it your best shot? We can be left thinking:

- *I care deeply about my work, but you want me to care deeper?*
- *I work long hours, but you want me to work even longer?*
- *I try to make the best decisions, but you want me to somehow make better ones?*

It is exasperating. It is excruciating. And it is killing us.

Dr Brené Brown cites the value of vulnerability as being at the core of human happiness and satisfaction. Brown's work spans more than

20 years with in-depth scientific studies, creating a worldwide movement. She defines vulnerability as uncertainty, risk and emotional exposure. In her book, *Daring Greatly*,[1] Brown says vulnerability is "the birthplace of love, belonging, joy, courage, empathy and creativity." However, we experience *excruciating vulnerability* when we feel exposed and uncertain. This is when fear and shame are fed, allowed to grow, and take over our modern decision-making abilities. To avoid these feelings, Brown says we numb ourselves by overeating (we are at record-high levels of obesity), over escaping (drug and alcohol abuse), over shopping (personal debt) and overdosing (prescription drug abuse).

This destructive behaviour cannot continue. We need to start looking at other ways to bring in high-performance results. This pressure-cooker, anxiety-inducing, exhausting expectation we place on ourselves and each other to always work harder is simply not sustainable. It may get us into an entry-level position. It may get us into our first management position. It may win us "the big account". It may even take our brand to number one in its category. But it has a limit. In this book, we will work through the diminishing returns of pure sweat and how we can close the book on hard work being the only way to get great results. Although this is relevant on an individual, team, departmental, organisational and industry level (and all will be referenced), our focus will be on team performance from a leader's perspective.

As soon as I tell people that working harder is not the answer, I get a sharp response. People even get offended and find it difficult to accept there is a different paradigm.

- *"If you're not working hard, then you're a bludger*!" (*Australian slang for being lazy)
- *"What do you mean? You want me to do nothing?"*
- *"If I'm not meant to work hard, then what am I meant to do?!"*

That last question is the right one to ask. Building the skill set that will get you to the top of your game and keep you there still requires a lot of hard work – but it's a different type of hard work. As you will see, it requires more discipline than pure effort.

Work doesn't have to be about survival.

To be super productive as a professional and as a leader, you need to understand the factors that keep you and those around you inspired, motivated and focused on creating new opportunities. You also need to know how to lead the external (team) and internal (self) environments.

The hard work is in the changes you need to make. Not in *what* you are doing, but *how* you are doing it.

The hard work is also in breaking life-long habits that no longer serve you. Research is required to figure out "what good looks like" in your workflow, your team's workflow, and your organisation as a whole. You will need to experiment with new ways of working, undergo some trial and error, be more mindful, and accept that you need to go slow to go quick. The journey requires a commitment to creating a new way of working that develops a beautiful cadence of rhythm, one that is repeatable, enjoyable and super rewarding.

Rhythm (The New Paradigm)

In the early stages of the 21st century, we face a clear challenge: there are finite resources.

During the 19th and 20th centuries, the Industrial Revolution thrived on the belief that there were endless oil, gas and coal reserves to dig up, process and consume. There were new territories to discover and the world was a vast place.

Now, we know our human impact is profound, and an ever-expanding world population is pushing the planet and its resources to the limit.

We increasingly feel this squeeze in our day-to-day lives and workplaces. Small businesses cannot play a game of attrition. Almost every small business in the world struggles with cash-flow, and an external influence or new competitor can wipe a small enterprise out very quickly. Corporate businesses, by definition, continuously require better outcomes using fewer resources to satisfy the stock market. This relentless drive for efficiency "no matter the cost", as long as that cost is not the business's bottom line, creates a pressure-cooker environment. Add to this the ever-present reality of global events, such as viruses, natural disasters and political changes in a globalised economy, and we are left knowing one thing: that every professional needs to set themselves up in a strong, robust, yet nimble team. If we don't, we face more and more pressure in our roles, as though the walls are closing in.

No amount of "working harder" can halt the onslaught of these pressures. Even if working longer and putting in more effort did help, our bodies and minds would struggle to keep it up. After one year, two years, five years or 10, no matter how resilient we are, we will break. I have seen this first hand with family members, colleagues and clients throughout the years.

Research backs this up, too. Stress levels have risen by 20% over the past three decades.[2] Mental health conditions for business leaders have also skyrocketed.[3] And, aside from the human cost, the level of disruption to organisations and entire industries is constantly speeding up – especially when the disruptors themselves are being disrupted.

Uber is a prime example of this. The on-demand ride service entered the American market in 2009 and the Australian market in 2012 as one of the first *sharing economy** models we have experienced, turning the taxi industry on its head. Yellow Cabs in New York City went from having some of the most valuable licenses in the world to worthless ones. In just 10 years, all sorts of ride-sharing companies have entered the market: Lyft, Ola, Taxify, DiDi and Grab, to name a few. All of them vie to gain drivers and passengers at better deals with their own new technologies. Uber basically created an industry, but it is already under strain from younger, more agile challengers.

This same stress occurs for many of us in our roles and teams, as younger professionals with a better understanding of new technologies emerge. More to the point, some technologies, like artificial intelligence (AI) and robotics, are wiping out a lot of our roles.

---

* Sharing economy: where people use their own goods or services and sell access to others in the community, usually via an online platform. Also called peer-to-peer (P2P).

In fact, a Korn Ferry survey found that technology is one of the key reasons why we feel increasingly stressed.[4] The professionals surveyed attributed their stress levels to:

- Pressure from their boss
- Keeping up with technology
- Increased workloads
- Interpersonal conflict
- Losing their job due to technology

All of us experience these pressures in one way or another. On an individual level, what can we do to overcome them? How do we not only identify future challenges but successfully navigate them and find the solutions?

One suggestion I would like to put to you is to alter your paradigm. Step back from the day-to-day challenges and see the bigger game you are playing.

Think about it in terms of a sailor. How do they navigate the seas? They understand the capability of their vessel. They research their routes, options and the weather. They know the currents and the unique set of conditions of their route. They're not on a motorboat, cruising down a river. In this case, they would simply put the throttle down and enjoy the wind in their hair. No, the sailor is in a highly dynamic environment where heavy winds blow, then they die down; where the quickest, most efficient route may include lots of zigs and zags. The sailor works with their crew and boat hard when the weather demands it, but will relax and consolidate when the weather calms.

A natural cycle occurs. Day to night. High wind to low wind. Rough seas to calm seas. Favourable currents to resistant currents. The sailor must work with these cycles. So, too, must business leaders. Many leaders are shocked and surprised when mistakes and problems arise. They had thought they were sailing down a river when they were really in the sea. We need to make sense of the patterns within this dynamic sea environment, so we can make effective decisions and solve problems.

Our bodies also have cycles called circadian rhythms. These are the daily physical, mental and behavioural changes we all experience. For example, we respond to the light of day and the dark of night. We sleep in cycles – from light sleep to REM (rapid eye movement) to deep sleep, which helps us recover and repair mentally and physically for the next day. We have monthly cycles, more obvious for women, but I am convinced (with no scientific basis) that men also go through a less-obvious monthly cycle. We are a part of this natural world, too, right?! We experience seasons through the year, and within our businesses, we have revenue cycles – high times and slow times.

Many of us operate within these cycles without thinking about them. Yet, we still resist the idea that we can't always go full throttle like the motorboat on the river. We forget – or don't want to admit – that we are on a boat on the high seas, and we must zig, zag, stop and go at different times, depending on the rhythms we are experiencing externally and internally. When we resist the rhythms, we create unnecessary work that prevents us from getting to our destination and hitting our targets and goals.

But when we synchronise with these rhythms, we can get to where we need to go without superfluously expending our limited resources. When a team understands its internal rhythms and members synchronise with each other, the many random, dynamic events they face become clear and make sense.

I feel that the first natural step for us as leaders is to understand these rhythms in the business we lead. This allows us to align our individual workflows with our environment. As a natural extension, we can begin the process of aligning our team members with this flow to create a strong structure that supports creativity, productivity and cohesion.

This new paradigm of the Rhythm Effect is one I have been sharing with businesses – and seeing great results. It can sound a little woo-woo at times, but have no doubts: decades of research (which I will share with you) have proven that concepts such as "being in the zone", "flow" and "rhythm" are legitimate performance concepts. There are many case studies of these concepts in action, providing giant leaps forward for professionals and their organisations. It is an exciting body of work to immerse yourself in but be warned: putting these principles into action can be confronting and require a lot of patience, time and energy. The payoff will be one of higher productivity, with more engagement and job satisfaction a result of higher achievement and closer relationships. Most of all, you will discover the beauty and power of agency coupled with impact. This is not only gratifying of itself, but it enables legacy – even in a small, local way.

Work doesn't have to be about survival. We don't have to operate in a way that increases friction and resistance in our teams, where we begrudge the challenges (and people) we are responsible for. Our work can be about enjoyment, achievement and deep engagement. It is possible for all of us, no matter how difficult, awkward or desperate our starting point is. And I have no doubt we can all achieve well beyond what we have done before. Rather than worrying about the finite resources we have to play with, we can focus on the infinite possibilities we can explore and achieve. As a partially reformed workaholic, I will share with you my experiences from the sporting arena, the consumer product industry, and my exposure to hundreds of businesses as an educator helping to develop the rhythm principles.

The implications of these principles are far-reaching and powerful. The Rhythm Effect is growing into a high-performing model for individuals, teams, departments and organisations. I am excited to show you what I have learnt about team leadership performance, and I look forward to continuing this conversation with you into the future.

Experts in Friction

"It's not the writing part that's hard. What's hard is the sitting down to write. What keeps us from sitting down is Resistance."
– Steven Pressfield, The War of Art

When pedalling a bicycle, the hardest part is usually the start. This is when maximum friction is felt. We have no momentum and need to do a lot of mental and physical work to get some forward movement and balance. We work hard for meagre results. But once we get going, we get some speed up, and it becomes easier to go fast with less effort.

Entering a new job or project is not dissimilar. Unfortunately, when processes are poor (or absent) and cultures of inconsistent communication and decision making are the norm, friction is sustained. In some cases, it gets worse. I believe we have become experts in managing these frictions rather than removing them and, in some cases, we have become experts in perpetuating them.

Frictions vary in the way they present, but our modern organisations are riddled with them. This creates a difficult and stressful situation, where finding rhythm and gaining synchronisation between our teams is near impossible. Friction, or "resistance", as Steven Pressfield describes it, is all around us. As leaders, if we can identify the main forms of friction, we can understand how to navigate beyond them and form our own momentum, flow and eventual rhythm.

Motivation and Friction

It's a typical Sunday evening on a typically hot Aussie day. I am lazing about after a weekend full of the usual pleasures: socialising, sport and time with my wife, Jana. As the sun goes down, I do what I do every Sunday evening: I turn my mind from my weekend escape to Monday. The trepidation of Monday…

Conference calls, reports and dealing with the huge agenda overhanging from the week before. It's not much different to the previous week, except the to-do-list is longer with a pinch of extra pressure. The dread builds. Anxiety creeps in as I anticipate and play out all the possibilities and think of the conversations I don't want to have. My energy levels are low, as I haven't slept well due to the weekend's binge drinking, and I ask myself: *"What story could I spin to take the day off?"*

It's tempting, but as a regional manager, it is not an option. My rational brain pipes up and reminds me that hiding under a blanket in bed for a day is not the answer. All that work will still be waiting for me, only with less time to do it. I decide to drag myself to work, put on a smiley and positive face, and do my best.

This scenario played out every weekend for years. What I didn't realise was that I wasn't the only person living with these feelings every Sunday. With a little research, I discovered that many people had the experience. In fact, a study by The Sleep Judge found that 81% of people experienced an elevated sense of anxiety on Sunday in anticipation of the week ahead.[5] This experience is called the *Sunday dread*, where anxiety starts mildly on a Sunday morning. Gradually, it builds momentum throughout the day to the point of serious anxiety symptoms, including headache, irritability, depressed mood, and a bad night's sleep, making Monday a serious trauma.

The contemporary workplace is riddled with anxiety and complexity. Every manager works tirelessly to manage themselves through these pressures, while desperately trying to keep their team members on track. When I work with general managers and executives in a facilitation or coaching setting, I find this theme is what commonly holds leaders and their teams back. The Sunday dread creates a snowball effect felt by leaders and professionals throughout the week, compromising productivity. It is self-feeding; an energy-depleting distraction that creates new, more potent forms of friction in our workplaces.

Motivation is an intangible beast. As a leader, it can be difficult to understand where the accountability lies when it comes to your team's motivation. If the company that employs your people doesn't give them a reason to buy-in, there will be a limit as to how much they care. But it is also up to the individual to find a purpose and passion within their role that relates to the company's vision.

Motivation experts like Dan Pink tell us it is the prospect of *mastery, autonomy and purpose* that lifts a professional's motivation. When team members experience this combination with clarity, their working days become fun filled and exciting instead of laborious and anxiety ridden. Not only is it a happier environment for workers, but it is much more gratifying as well. If we, as leaders, provide an environment for this, our workplaces will burst with highly motivated people. I think there is merit in this idea, but, like many concepts, it is all in the implementation.

Here are a few things I have learnt about motivation:

1. Motivation is Deeply Personal

Applying blanket rules to your situation and team can be useful at times, but they're unlikely to have a lasting effect. Michael Vaughan, the former English cricket captain who famously won the Ashes against the dominant Australian juggernaut led by Steve Waugh in 2005, used advice from his father to motivate his team. Vaughan's father said, "If you're going to be a leader, you need to know who you are leading."

This speaks to the idea of getting to know your people. I spent years pretending to get to know my clients and team players in the corporate environment. I would ask about their weekends and families, politely smiling and nodding while thinking, "Get on with it, we have work to do!"

It is shameful to admit this, but I don't think I am alone. We are all rushed, busy and under pressure. It's easy to find ourselves partaking in social norms with little investment or intent to truly listen. As understandable as this is, I came to realise this approach is flawed. For example, it took me a whole year to figure out that one of my assistant managers was more interested in time off than money. All it would have taken was one good, solid conversation over lunch to understand this, and it would have meant one year less of absenteeism, infighting with other staff, and friction in our relationship, which was a strain on both of us and knocked us out of rhythm.

Removing assumptions and taking the time to check in on and be present with others shows that we care. It also gives us a strong understanding of our troops, so we can make better decisions that keep our people "up for it".

2. Motivation is Not Set and Forget

If you think all it takes to understand the motivations of your staff members and clients is a one-off chat to ask about their favourite wine, incentive of choice and whether they prefer email or text communication, you will be sorely disappointed. Motivation is not a shopping list of items to tick off. People are complex, and the triggers that help them perform are also complex. Our teams are dynamic, and if we, as leaders, do not keep up with the cascade of changes, we can find ourselves becoming irrelevant very quickly.

By making it your business to understand how your people are developing, you'll be one step ahead in finding the right opportunities to keep your people stimulated, challenged and connected to the business.

Think of it as a dinner party. As the leader, you are the host. It is your job to not only have a good time but also to attend to your guests. Welcome them and make them feel comfortable. Make sure they know each other and the environment. Engage in conversation with everyone throughout the night and listen to their stories. Ask lots of questions and be present when listening to their answers. Create space for group conversations while controlling the timing and structure of the evening. Remember, the group looks to you for their meal, much like your team looks to you for guidance, information, decisions and resources.

By consistently engaging with all team members and understanding the problems they're trying to solve, you'll keep everyone's motivation high and focused.

3. Motivation is Hindered by Teams

This may seem counterintuitive. How can it be that being placed in a team can lower people's motivation? This may be especially difficult to understand if you thrive on group learning and doing things with others.

The answer lies in a phenomenon called *social loafing*. In 1890, Max Ringelman, a French professor of agricultural engineering, conducted a study that asked subjects to pull ropes as individuals, and then as members of a group. Ringelman found that subjects exerted less effort in a group situation than when they performed individually. This study was repeated many times, yielding the same results.[6]

Social loafing happens when we think our efforts won't make much difference when we are in a group environment; therefore, there's no need to try as hard. We fundamentally have a lowered motivation to perform well when we are in a team versus when we are alone. In a group, there is room to hide and shy away from trying or taking responsibility for tasks. There is a low risk of being found out for "slacking off", as the group covers diminished effort.

Making matters worse is the fact that in these studies when people were told they were being paired with high performers, they did not do any better. In fact, they tried even less! Think about how this may play out in your team. Not only do you have people who don't try as hard as they would if they were working alone; you also have people who perform at an even lower level when they work alongside high-performing teammates.

Understanding that friction is constant holds us in good stead to take responsibility and have agency over our destination.

How long is it until the high performer wakes up to this? What will the high performer do when they realise others are not pulling their weight? Their performance may sink to the level of everyone else, or they'll stop performing altogether. As a leader, you need to wake up to the fact this is likely happening in your team right now.

The realisation that people are less likely to give their all when grouped together is an important one for leaders. By knowing it happens, we can put relevant actions in place to snuff it out completely, or at least keep it to a minimum. Social loafing is a point of friction that halts individual and team rhythm. Having one unmotivated person in a team is enough to upset the rhythm of a collective workflow. And if a leader suffers from lowered motivation, it quickly spreads throughout the team. Acknowledging this and taking steps to target it is essential to creating a high-performing team with ongoing rhythm.

Competition, Customers and Friction

Most businesses play in the business to consumer (B2C) and/or business to business (B2B) markets. There are two variations of this: a *vertical business model*, where a business owns the complete supply chain, and a *horizontal business model*, where a business sells wholesale to clients who have their own points of distribution. Some businesses do all the above simultaneously!

This creates a complex business environment for all stakeholders, not to mention a difficult scenario when marketing and delivering to specific target markets. This situation is not new, and many executive teams have been working through their natural cycles of strategy to find the best growth opportunities. But shifts in market needs and expectations have shot through the roof in recent times.

Salesforce, a global market-leading CRM software company, published some startling statistics in its 2018 State of The Connected Customer report.[7] A double-blind survey of more than 6,700 business buyers and consumers was conducted in the major markets worldwide. It was found that 76% of respondents felt it was easier than ever to take their business elsewhere. When you marry this with the fact that 67% of customers say their expectations of a "good experience" are higher than ever before, we can see that earning (and keeping) loyal customers has never been tougher.

There is an increasing amount of options and scepticism in the market. Every day, it seems a new platform is announced on social media, giving consumers new ways of exploring, discovering, shopping and buying products. Ten years ago, there was no *fast fashion* in many world markets. Now, brands like H&M, Zara and Uniqlo dominate the fashion markets and are sucking up huge chunks of finite raw material in the supply chain of textiles.

Another example is the shared economy, as discussed earlier. The battle between traditional taxi companies and ridesharing companies like Uber, Ola, Lyft, etc., means consumers are demanding a better service at a lower price. This makes for a promiscuous consumer with ever-increasing demands.

Businesses that think they can rest on their laurels for a year, three years or a decade will be left behind. Nandu Nandkishore and James Michael Lafferty, from London Business School, write that the lifespan of a company has reduced significantly.[8] In the 1920s, the average lifespan of a company was 90 years. In the 1950s, that number decreased to 60 years. Now, it is a meagre 17 years. If that number doesn't frighten you as much as it frightens me, then please throw some ice-cold water on your face and wake up! Nandkishore and Lafferty cite two main reasons for such high failure rates in the modern business environment:

1. Competition Bites

New, young up-starts come in and turn the contemporary customer's head. They have less to lose and are hungry. They woo customers with their audacity, while established companies fall into a false sense of security, believing their loyal customers will never leave. The taxi war is a standout example. When Uber came into the market, it encouraged its drivers to supply customers with bottled water, mints and music options. The paying public loved this. They felt like they were being ferried around by their own private drivers at a cheaper rate, while the old cabs still struggled to pick the best route to get you where you wanted to go!

Understanding what the contemporary consumer wants and needs (even when they may not know what they need) is difficult at the best of times. Providing the best and most competitive solution can be even trickier. In marketing terms, we call this a product's *focus of appeal*. Being the front-of-mind brand is an ongoing game none of us can relax in.

Ask yourself: What is my favourite airline? What is my favourite sportswear brand? What are my three favourite restaurants in my town? Now, think about the hundreds of competitors in each of these fields that you did not immediately consider. This is the reality for all players in the market. And it exists for the market you and your team operate in. It even exists in the good, old "war for talent" we find ourselves in when recruiting. Competition is always there, and it is always developing in new and different ways. Be ready for it, or suffer the effects of the extra friction when trying to achieve your goals.

2. Distraction

Companies often focus on the wrong things. Global CEOs and boards constantly make decisions to satisfy important economic stakeholders. This means that often, the simple things get missed, like the customer and their ever-increasing demand for better and more personalised services. David Jones and Myer, the department store giants of Australia, have enjoyed a century of trying to beat each other in the yearly fashion/marketing/Christmas window wars. But in the past two decades, there has been a massive shift in buyer habits towards e-commerce. David Jones and Myer both reacted late to this trend, and their execution of online retail was poor, to say the least. As we enter the second decade of the 21st century, they continue to struggle to patch together an omi-channel experience the modern shopper wants to engage with.

These two retail giants spent too much attention on unimportant tools, initiatives and trends. They took their eye off the consumer and are paying heavily for it. Myer's stock price plummeted from $1.27 a share (Mar 2015) to $0.28 a share (Mar 2020). This downward trajectory resulted from generations of senior executives investing in outdated and irrelevant strategies, adding to the friction they already faced.

Spending time and resources on poor strategies and focusing on "trends" that are really just fads are great ways to work hard for little gain. Becoming detached and disconnected from the people you serve is a dangerous game, and will leave everyone (including yourself) drained, fatigued and unmotivated to keep pushing while the proverbial ship sinks.

Rapid Change and Friction

Not only are customer expectations and fickleness at an all-time high, but the general market is changing rapidly at unprecedented levels.

In Adelaide, I grew up doing two things: playing sport and drinking beer. Yes, I studied and worked in between, but my main focus was on those two activities. They complemented each other in the sense that I went out and drank with my teammates, forming deep relationships that are strong to this day. They also hindered each other, as drinking beer on a Saturday night after bowling 20-30 overs in scorching heat did not enhance my recovery. Nonetheless, it was a part of a young bloke's experience growing up in Adelaide. Our usual haunts comprised three key locations on and around Rundle Street, dubbed the Cooper's Triangle: The Austral (aka. The Nostril), The Exeter (aka. The X), and The Crown and Anchor (aka. The Cranker), which all served the locals' favourite brand of beer – Coopers.

Coopers is a family-owned business to this day. Many South Australians are proud of the brand, and it is still considered a huge success story for the state. When I lived in the UK, I would occasionally spend a ridiculous amount of money on a stubby of Coopers at the odd pub that stocked it, out of pure sentimentality (as you do when far from home). Now

I'm based in Melbourne, and it warms my heart to see Coopers signs outside many pubs around town. Those of us who grew up in South Australia loved Coopers because it represented a real beer; a brand that had soul compared to West End, the other locally brewed beer that represented low mass-market quality. Recently, however, Coopers has found itself in a bit of a pickle.

Over the past decade, the craft beer industry has blossomed. In fact, not only has it become a category of the beer industry, it has become its own industry. In Australia, craft beer is now a $604.8 million industry that has experienced 8.4% growth in the years 2014–19. This is made even more impressive by the fact that brewing beer is a scale game, where global corporates dominate (five brewers control approximately half the world's global beer volume).[9]

Why is this a problem for Coopers? It used to be the under-dog beer brand, known for its family values and being the small, relatable business for the conscientious consumer. In 2012, Coopers celebrated its 150th anniversary, and is now the only wholly Australian-owned major brewery, producing 76.8 million litres of beer annually. But somehow, Coopers became part of the establishment. The micro-breweries popping up everywhere now represent the "local" beers that locals want to support.

The disruptor has become the disrupted. Coopers is not big enough to weather this storm. It does not have the clout of Lion Nathan or Asahi, and it has lost its unique agility and positioning in the market as a challenger brand. In the words of Coopers Brewery managing director Dr Tim Cooper, "We are in no-man's land." In the 2018–19 financial year, Coopers registered a $23.1 million drop in profits and an $11 million loss from the previous year. The brand has no choice but to face up to this new challenge in an already high-risk industry.

All of us face new challenges and changes in our categories. Online learning and the *flipped classroom model* have changed education forever (as has Google!). Universities and everyone in the professional development industry must grapple with this shift to remain relevant.

World cricket is also facing unprecedented change, as Test cricket (the pinnacle of the sport) has never had such low crowd attendances. The business model is under severe strain. The introduction of one-day cricket and Twenty20 cricket has brought more eyeballs to the sport, but now these versions of the game are cannibalising talent and marketing dollars. The world's power brokers of cricket will need to constantly balance the shifting sands of the sporting horizon.

As leaders, the ever-increasing changes we face in our industries require agility and attention. Otherwise, we will be on the wrong side of the *17-year business lifespan*. Keeping up with rapid change requires vigilance and deep engagement. It takes effort and care, which can be fatiguing, especially when top-table leadership focuses on nothing else but hitting quarterly business targets to satisfy shareholders. Trying to maintain strong levels of motivation in these high-pressure environments can be a leader's worst nightmare. When the market shifts or a younger, sexier competitor swan in and steals your customers (and talent), it can be devastating. No matter how hard we work, more change is coming, and we must be ready for it. We need to be up for the challenge, and we need our people to be all in. Easier said than done, but it is a challenge we can prepare for and steel our people for.

These are the constant forces we live with; elements of friction that restrict team progress. These external pressures cannot be controlled, but they can be monitored, discussed and acted upon.

Currently, we are experiencing unprecedented weather patterns (or lack thereof!). So, if we turn back to our sailor navigating the high seas, he or she needs to be prepared for unseasonal storms, extreme wind conditions, changing currents, and so on. There is a constant stream of opportunities and challenges to act upon to keep the boat and crew on course, safe and stable. It is up to the sailor and crew to do this in a way that causes no harm or damage, using the least amount of resources.

Understanding that friction is a constant in our businesses and teams holds us in good stead for taking responsibility and having agency over our destination. This is critical for leaders and their teams to achieve rhythm. Knowing we have the ability to manoeuvre through our challenges helps us to not only get to our destination but to get there in style, without loss or sacrifice. We can surf our own momentum, where big, daunting waves no longer threaten to capsize us; they merely bounce off our hull.

The Cost of Hard Work

*"When we play with a finite mindset in an infinite game, the odds increase
that we will find ourselves in a quagmire, racing through the will and
resources we need to keep playing."*
– Simon Sinek, The Infinite Game

When playing South Australian grade cricket for East Torrens, there was
one simple exercise we had to do: run around the oval non-stop for an
hour. The challenge was to see how many laps we could do.

This was my worst nightmare. I didn't want to do it, I wasn't interested in
doing it, and did I mention that I didn't want to do it?! With no choice in
the matter, I set off and jogged at a pathetic pace compared to many
of my teammates. That didn't bother me. What bothered me was the
blister forming on my foot. I didn't want to stop, as that would have been
too much for my fragile ego to handle, but I also didn't want to create
a problem that would prevent me from getting ready to play cricket at
the start of the season.

I voiced my concern to my coach, who told me what I needed to do.
"Keep going, do what you can!" I walked and lightly jogged for the rest
of the activity. The most challenging part of this experience was the
constant chatter in my head; not just during the run, but throughout
most of my pre-season training. I was always telling myself that I was
rubbish, that training was really hard, and that I couldn't wait for it to be
over. Without realising it, I was making a tough situation even tougher
for myself. This manifested physically (I was more tired, which reduced
my ability to perform), but I was unconscious of it at the time.

Exhaustion Lowers Rhythm

1. Personal Exhaustion

Pre-season training at East Torrens was not my favourite time. There are some of us who find running gruelling, boring and generally difficult, and pre-season consisted of a lot of running. I despised it.

I was about 20 years old at the time and in the best shape of my life. Standing approximately 6'3", I was thickset, strong and developing. Yet, I didn't realise how tense I was. It was only when I did another running drill next to one of the "good old boys" of the club that it became evident to me that I was seriously tight and wound up. During one running exercise, I was partnered with Greg "Quinny" Quinn, a club legend and well known around the South Australian club cricket scene. At that time, he was the C-grade captain, a leader within the playing squad and a real crack up, too – always joking and bringing a smile to everyone's faces.

During this running drill, we formed two lines next to each other. Quinny was my partner. In this formation, we had to jog for about 500 metres; then when the whistle went, we had to sprint at about 80% capacity. It was a fitness drill but also a teamwork drill. We had to keep in formation, and there was no out – you had to come along with the team no matter what. Quitting was simply not an option. Running next to Quinny was the best thing for me. He didn't say a word the whole time, but what I heard next to me was a huge wake-up call that has stayed with me to this day. As I panted and puffed my way through the sprints with short, sharp breaths, Quinny, who was about 20 years older than me, took slow, deep breaths. It was like listening to lapping waves hitting the shore, then flowing back into the ocean. I could also hear his face. I know this sounds weird, but I could hear how relaxed his cheeks, lips and skin were. If you watch slow-motion front-on footage of 100-metre sprinters, you'll see what I mean. There is complete relaxation in their face and entire body. When I compared this to what I was doing, I realised how much tension I was running with – and it wasted a considerable amount of energy and compromised my performance. On top of this, I was fatiguing myself mentally, as I constantly told myself I could not do these types of drills well.

That day became a defining moment in my short sporting career. To this day, I hear Quinny's slow, relaxed breathing whenever I am in a high-performance scenario. It is a great reminder.

In our modern-day workplaces, I see a similar tension to what held me back in my pre-season training all those years ago. As an external consultant coming into businesses, I can see it on people's faces, in how they walk and in how they speak to each other. In 1971, Albert Mehrabian published the book, *Silent Messages*, in which he discussed the 7-38-55% rule. Mehrabian's studies found that people overwhelmingly deduce their feelings, attitudes and beliefs about what someone says not by the words they speak, but by the speaker's body language and tone of voice. Mehrabian quantified this tendency:[10]

- Spoken words account for 7% of personal communication
- Tone of voice accounts for 38% of personal communication
- Body language accounts for 55% of personal communication

This study has been replicated many times with minor variances. I talk about it in all sorts of training programs. It is a useful way to discuss the importance of our physical signals when working with others, rather than just obsessing about the content of our meetings, speeches and conversations. Some evidence suggests that Mehrabian's percentages are not correct, or are relevant only in Western society. I acknowledge this, while also acknowledging that our body language says a lot! We all watch and react to it every day, consciously and subconsciously.

Clenched jaws are in our office spaces everywhere. Stress levels are rising. This is not only something leaders need to manage for better team performance; it needs to be tackled in its own right, as stress costs energy. The mental stamina required in professional settings is already high. When we fight growing tension and stress, it exhausts us even more, and we can find ourselves in ever-increasing deficits.

Stress is leading to exhaustion, making it difficult for people to make good decisions, be productive, focus their attention and perform over a sustained period. And it makes it almost impossible to get into a groove, set up cycles of working and introduce rhythm into the way we work. We are exhausted mentally and physically, and so are our whole organisations. A massage or weekend away may help recharge the batteries, but discovering a way of working that is not mentally exhausting would be of much greater benefit.

2. Corporate Exhaustion

No matter what business you are in or the size of your organisation, there is one global truth: there are never enough resources. Or, put another way, no one has a bottomless pit of resources. Yet, in my 15-year corporate career, I constantly saw (and was part of) budget adjustments and budget re-allocations when results did not come in on plan.

There are practical reasons for this. Boards and chief executives need to set expectations for shareholders and investors and strategise for the future. Unfortunately, a big part of this process can involve massaging and fudging the results. People tend to cover their backside to protect their ego or to avoid being the scapegoat. It can become a political game, where tensions run high, and people's blood pressure runs even higher.

This process always left me wondering, *"Who is paying for this?"* When I worked in the corporate arena, there was always so much tension and importance placed on delivering business results across all departments. But when the results did not come in, where did the businesses get the extra cash from? Of course, the answer is that they didn't. I was once part of a corporate business that suffered so many poor results, locations got shut down, and people were let go. If you have been around for long enough or speak to enough people, you'll see this happens quite often. Businesses that suffer from internal and external pressures chew up resources they can ill afford. No one is immune to this, and when resources are taken for granted, empires can crash. As Ernest Hemingway once wrote, *"How did you go bankrupt?"*

"Two ways. Gradually, then suddenly." In a broader context, I feel that everything in life happens gradually, and then suddenly.

Another area that exhausts company resources is the *revolving door of recruitment*, referring to the constant cost of people leaving and entering a business. If I could have one professional superpower that could help organisations find and keep "good staff", I would be the richest man on the planet. Professionally, hardly a week that goes by when I am not asked by a human resources professional or manager if I know "anyone good" who is looking for a new opportunity. Yet, on the other side of the coin, rarely do I go to a barbecue or dinner party where someone at the table isn't having such a hard time at work that they are actively looking for a new job. A huge disconnect exists between employees and employers, with the gap seemingly widening.

Recently, Robert Half Australia conducted its annual survey of 460 hiring managers. It was reported that one in seven workers was actively looking for a job and that more than two-thirds of employers had seen an increase in staff turnover in the past three years.[11] This has a dramatic effect on productivity levels throughout organisations and creates a major cost for businesses that continuously recruit, onboard, train and exit-manage staff. It is a drain on the company's bottom line and on leaders, too. When combined with the constant market forces discussed earlier, such as the battle for consumer attention and market share, these ongoing costs become a real handicap that can push a business towards extinction.

When our resources are drained, we can fall. Any chance of setting up cycles, programs and systems that seamlessly synchronise to take a business unit from strength to strength is simply impossible. It is like being a parent to a newborn and operating on no sleep. You can adjust, do your best and jack yourself up on energy drinks and coffee. But the energy deficit will build, mistakes will be made, memory will fail, and there is an expiry date on how long a human can operate like that.

Margaret Heffernan, a technology CEO, writes in her book, *Beyond Measure*,[12] that IT companies go through a period called *crunch time*.

Everything in life
happens gradually,
and then suddenly.

This is when a development team makes one last push to deliver its project on time and go live. Everyone works around the clock, and every sinew of the business's resources is stretched to the limit. The project then gets delivered, and everyone crashes. They take holidays, time out, and generally wind down to recover. Heffernan warns that some people get this wrong and unwittingly operate in crunch time mode all the time. One example cited is Electronic Arts (EA Sports). In 2004, it set a standard that employees would work eight-hour days, six days a week. This quickly turned into longer days, and the unwritten expectation became seven days a week. A class-action lawsuit was filed against the company and was settled in 2006, resulting in business practices being duly amended. The interesting thing about this story is that the performance of the teams working these long hours was poor. Their ability to solve problems went through the floor, and they made more mistakes and created more re-work.

A team's ability to move forward productively and profitably is severely hindered when there is a constant exhaustion of resources. Embracing the rhythms of our industry, location and revenue cycles is far more effective than working really hard for longer. In fact, working more is counter-productive, and you could argue that companies pay large sums of overtime for worse results!

Breeding Resentment, Not Rhythm

In my world, there are two types of people: those who cheat at board games and those who do not. There is nothing like getting together with family or friends for some food and drinks and having a laugh over a classic board game. It's always good for a giggle. One guarantee is there will be a few people in the group or a team who insist on cheating. They'll give each other sly looks while us non-cheaters naively wonder why we are losing every round. At some point, I will finally clock onto it, take the righteous, judgmental stance, and condemn the cheaters. Usually, at this point, the cheaters become even happier with the chaos they have created, and it is all laughed off.

What I didn't realise for a long time was that it's the non-cheaters who create more resentment than the cheaters. Multiple studies show that the people who do the right thing all the time are a real turn off. The "goody two-shoes" seem to get more backlash from the group than those who cheat. Researchers cite two reasons for this: the virtuous make everyone else feel inferior, and groups believe that those who always play by the rules are inadvertent "rule breakers" because they don't conform to the unwritten norms everyone else plays by.[13]

I find this fascinating, and it explains why hard-working people with good intentions keep finding themselves in situations of resentment and friction. A common reaction to this is to work harder, always lead by example and show that they never ask anyone to do anything they do not do themselves. This can lead to the team becoming even more resentful while creating a deep resentment from the leader towards their staff.

Not only have I experienced this myself throughout my career; I have coached and mentored many others through this type of scenario. My clients will often hear me use the term "funky". You know when you set out with a clean and clear plan, then everything gets a bit muddled along the way? In the '80s and '90s, if something was funky, it was cool or hip. But these days when something is funky, it means it has gone off and stinks a little. It is another way to understand why pure, hard work is not the answer. In this type of funky environment, more hard work on the leader's part will drive resentment further and deepen the gaping hole in the communication and culture of the team. My observation is that this is where micro-management seeds from: an over-enthusiasm to see the job done properly coming from a good intention but expressed in a deeply flawed way.

When we can see what is really happening and why people act the way they do, we can start to take a different approach. Instead of working harder and leading by example in a more obvious and desperate way, a leader has other options. A starting point may be to stop. Stop working so much. Stop being the hero of your own story. Instead, remember why you are playing in the first place: to have fun with the people around you. When I am at a dinner party playing a board game, am I there to win? No. Am I there to have fun with my nearest and dearest? Yes. All of a sudden, this change in perspective opens a world of possibilities, a different dialogue, and a new way forward that impacts everyone's experience.

The leader's job is not to be the best performer. It is not to do everything others do not do. And it certainly is not a leader's job to point out all the problems with people's work. These things only create more work, resentment and friction. They drag team performance down and, once again, cost the company money and reputation.

Eroding Belief

A question my dad has asked me a few times is: *"Why didn't you make it to the Australian cricket team?"* It's a great question, and one I am sure many people who played at grade and first-class level have come to terms with. We usually say, *"I wasn't good enough."*

This, unfortunately, is a cop out. It is a half-truth and a huge over-simplification that deflects the true answer.

The answer I have given to myself and my family is that I started too late. I grew up playing country cricket on concrete pitches with synthetic matting and volunteer coaching. I was about 20 years old before I graduated to grade cricket played on turf and became part of the cricketing system. Then, over the next few years, I worked my way to A-grade cricket (one level below state or first class) and earned myself a professional club contract in the UK.

During this period, I was lucky enough to train with the Australian Test Team as a net bowler, which was one of the best sporting experiences of my life. I did this for a few years, and it was a lot of fun. I also represented Cambridgeshire at under-21 level, which was an incredible honour. But then, in my early to mid-20s, I had a choice to make. The truth was that I never intended to pursue the journey to the top. I never thought it was possible for me. I never believed I was good enough, so I copped out before I had a chance. Before you throw me a pity party, please know that I enjoyed many opportunities, played at a standard many never get to (which I am proud of), and ended up staying in the UK for 10 years, where I had countless extraordinary experiences. In the end, my decision to move away from the sport and pursue a meaningful career turned out really well for me. What I would like to highlight is that when I look back at my cricket career, I realise I played a large portion of it in a state of fear. It was rare that I felt in control, relaxed and grounded.

One example of this was my bowling follow through. Fast bowling is all about momentum. A bowler runs in to gain pace and forward thrust, which transitions into the ball as it is released. The bowler then runs down the pitch after they let go of the ball – this is called a *"follow through"*. My run-up was from 17 paces. I was a big guy who generated a lot of force in my delivery stride. I would release the ball from a high angle because of my height, but then I would only take one or two abrupt strides after letting go of the ball. I stopped, like a golfer or tennis player taking a shot and then stopping their stroke once the ball was hit. For me, that meant I lost speed, accuracy, feel and control. It put me in a reactionary situation and, overall, it created a mental and physical tension that set me up for a negative spiral of performance if anything minor went wrong.

As someone who has coached across many sports and is a conscientious learner, the question is: why would I not relax and focus on being more fluid in my action and follow through? The answer is that I was worried. I was in a mini state of panic. As soon as I let go of the ball, I was worried about what would happen next. And when things didn't go well, I became more tense and agitated, and guess what would happen? I'd be pulled out of the bowling attack and asked to take a breather to reset and, hopefully, come back later refreshed.

One day when I was bowling, one of our English imports, Jonathan Finch, was fielding in the position next to me, mid off. Finchy is still a good friend of mine. He is now the sporting director of women's cricket for the ECB (English and Wales Cricket Board). On this particular day, Finchy handed me the ball before I bowled each ball, giving me encouragement. He shouted, *"Believe, Junior! Believe!"* I remember it like yesterday. The calls of "believe, believe" were insightful.

Why is this day so memorable? And what is the difference between a person believing they can get a result and believing they can't?

I see what this looks like in our teams at work. We are handed down very difficult targets from global and regional hierarchies, and deep down, we struggle to understand how we can achieve them. Sometimes, we privately mock these targets and laugh them off with a deeply uncomfortable awkwardness, before putting on a brave face and giving it our best. Sometimes, we grit our teeth and forge ahead using the old blood, sweat and tears routine. Sometimes, we push back and have heated, robust discussions about why the work is not possible. Ultimately, we start from a place of disbelief. An over-riding doubt prevails that the target is not possible to achieve.

Simon Sinek calls this the *finite mindset*. Like me and my bowling, the finite mindset never truly believes. That is the real reason I never made it to the top. It is an uncomfortable reality that accurately answers my father's question, and I can see it in people's eyes everywhere I go. It is the same look I see when I facilitate robust conversations for business teams, and on the faces of my university students towards the end of every semester before final submissions are due. People are in their own version of a never-ending crunch time, and they are uncertain of the outcome. There is an underlying panic. They do not believe they will make it or are good enough to achieve the goal.

When we are in this state, there is no chance of creating and sustaining a rhythmic way of working. There is no chance of setting ourselves up to deliver high-standard results that will build on themselves. And it is unlikely we can achieve any goals without using a disproportionate amount of human or company resources.

---

* For those who did not grow up with me, you may not know that my nickname is Junior, as I am the youngest of two brothers. I look a lot like my brother Anthony, so I was simply named Junior by our mates – it stuck!

Emma Murray is a high-performance mindfulness coach who has worked with top athletes, including race car driver Scott McLaughlin and the Richmond Football Club. Murray says anxiety-induced insomnia can directly cause physical performance problems, such as cramping during races and matches. The worry of not performing becomes a cornerstone of underperformance.[14]

In my experience, coming from a place of belief is critical to gathering momentum and generating strong performance delivery and replication (rhythm). When we nurture our self-belief, we avoid the needless expenditure of nervous energy, time and effort for little return. As leaders, we cannot afford to have a mindset full of self-doubt. It undermines our credibility, but more importantly, if we allow others to feel we do not believe in them, we are doomed before we begin.

When we speak with conviction and instil the belief in our teams that achievement is within grasp, we lay down the foundation for getting wins on the board (even if they are small). These wins create belief in each individual and the team. An environment of belief becomes the norm, and the tension, distractions and indecisiveness dissipate. Belief is essential for teams and leaders to achieve rhythm in their workflows, and to synchronise teammates and external stakeholders.

Eroding Trust

As Warren Buffett said, *"It takes 20 years to build a reputation and five minutes to ruin it."* There is no doubt that when trust is lost, things are not the same. For leaders of most organisations, trust heavily influences results in two key areas:

1. External Relationships

When clients are unhappy with a service or product, they usually walk. It varies from industry to industry, and from B2C to B2C, but we know that many consumers will simply move on rather than give feedback. According to 1Financial Training Services, 96% of unhappy customers don't complain, and 91% of those will take their business elsewhere.[15] There are no second chances, and no opportunity to make up whatever perceived wrong has occurred.

If I reflect on myself as a consumer, I know how I feel in such situations. I have enough troubles and challenges in my life where I need to have confrontational conversations and manage conflict. The last thing I want to do is have a confrontational conversation with the waiter at a restaurant, the person passing me jeans to try on in a shop, or an insurance company call centre. Most of the time, I want to avoid a conversation altogether and will take the path of least resistance by quietly going elsewhere.

To go back to Warren Buffett's point, it does not take much for us to lose trust. It doesn't always come down to one event or big moment, either. Foxtel, NewsCorp's subscription TV offering, had dominated the Australian pay-TV landscape for decades but is now suffering such a fate. In August 2019, NewsCorp chief executive Robert Thomson revealed to shareholders that the parent company would inject a further $200 million into the TV business, bringing total Foxtel loans to $500 million. This was to cover the rise in costs of sporting events, which coincided with a 30% fall in revenue compared to the previous financial year. The key metric hurting Foxtel was its subscriber churn rate (the number of subscribers who cancel), which was reported at 14.7% in the three months to 30th June 2019, up from 12.5% in the same period the previous year. Concurrently, the average user revenue also fell by 1%.[16]

These are worrying signs of a business that has lost trust. Foxtel is competing with online-streaming services that previously did not exist. New players are coming into the market and winning programming rights, with substantial licensing fees driving up Foxtel's expenditure. And its user experience is declining, as subscribers who are used to getting all the best sporting events, newest movies and unique category programming are being charged more than ever. Netflix, Stan, Optus, Apple TV and Freeview (amongst many other online-streaming services) have changed the way people consume their content, leaving

Foxtel looking and feeling like a dinosaur in an industry they once dominated.

Foxtel has been reduced to heavily discounting its offerings wherever it can, and it is marketing heavily to find new subscribers. This makes current subscribers feel even more short changed. Over a decade, Foxtel has lost the trust of its core base as the home entertainment package that can meet the entire family's needs. The business no longer delivers on its promises, and consumers have stopped trusting Foxtel and its representatives on the other end of the phone.

If we do not breed trust in the marketplace, we breed doubt. And with doubt comes more work; a need to work harder to hit targets, rather than stepping into a new, more efficient paradigm of work. If we rely on deals, promotions, discounts and gimmicks to keep our businesses going, then the costs will need to be covered elsewhere. If we rely on the hope that old systems will hold up, that reduced workforces can pull through, that reduced company budgets will be enough, or that a new fancy software system will change our fortunes, then we're in trouble.

Simply hoping things will be OK is defensive rather than offensive. It also erodes our confidence that we can penetrate the marketplace, and when that happens, there is no way we can create any rhythm or forward momentum. If we don't work on nurturing trust in our external relationships, we rob ourselves of the chance to have agency over our destination and to work with the people we enjoy working with. When we do not have someone to serve (or we do not like who we serve), we enter a highly volatile position where trust, in any form, is on a knife's edge.

I believe all of us have the opportunity every day to build trust in our relationships with our customers and stakeholders. This book aims to give every leader and their teams the skills and tools they need to build trust, particularly in the face of competing priorities and pressures.

2. Internal Relationships

For every micro-moment we don't trust our colleagues, a cost is incurred. Time is lost, work is duplicated, and mistakes are made. There is an old saying that goes, *"Trust. Once you get, it's priceless. But once you lose it, you are useless."*

Small cracks in trust become gaping chasms. It can happen quickly, too – sometimes, in a moment. But often, it is a quiet, cancerous, invisible and intangible threat that lingers in and around our offices and online communications. Sitting there. Slowly pulling. Slowly creating lag. Weight. Consuming energy, time and money. Consuming thought and mental space. Creating doubt and, eventually, showing up in tangible outcomes, such as revenue results and other key performance indicators (KPIs).

We see the effects of internal trust erosion in professional football clubs, too. When a team is struggling and in line for relegation, it can set off a chain reaction of events. Supporters stop attending games, and the ones who do attend are disgruntled. This makes sponsors unhappy. And when ticket sales go down, the club's management and ownership get worried and impatient from a financial point of view. Executives are pushed to work harder to get better results. They apply pressure to the football department. The manager of the playing staff feels the pressure more than anyone. It's lonely, and there is a squad full of players to keep happy while trying to figure out a way to get them to perform. Winning points becomes excruciatingly difficult, and every missed opportunity exacerbates the pressure everyone feels. With every part of the club at breaking point, the manager is sacked. This changes very little, except to create more fear within the organisation. A distinct signal is sent to all staff: no one trusts anyone. Everyone's job is on the line, and everyone is trying to save their skin. In effect, every employee, from the canteen chef to the captain, is rendered useless to each other. The one thing they feared, relegation, becomes a certainty.

A recent PricewaterhouseCoopers (PwC) Global CEO Survey found that the world's leading CEOs agree that trust is essential. More than

55% of the CEOs surveyed believed a lack of trust within an organisation threatened growth more than any other factor.[17] The ability to maintain and increase trust every day is a determinant of success. Leaders who allow team trust to erode through small, seemingly unimportant gestures enable cliques to form, segregation amongst staff, and possible disdain down the line.

Guarding and promoting trust is a cornerstone of leadership. Yet I can testify to more than two decades of witnessing leaders, especially those in senior management positions, saying and doing things that completely disregard this. That is not to say that these leaders were bad people or in any way incompetent. It is to highlight the pressure and strain under which we can find ourselves, and how competing priorities can leave us feeling as though we have no other choice. When we can navigate these moments with more grace, openness and vulnerability, we can set up a loop of trust. Since it is so difficult to cultivate and so elusive to find as an employee, trust is one of the most valuable assets a team can have.

In Australia, trusting the person next to you with your life is known as *mateship*. It originates from a history of military soldiers looking after each other in the most desperate environments imaginable. In our contemporary workplaces, we need to be able to trust that our processes and systems work. We also need to trust that our teammates behind those processes are doing what needs to be done. People must trust that their fellow team members will be there for them when things go sideways. A leader who cultivates this kind of trust will make great leaps forward.

When leaders and team members deeply trust each other and know everyone is delivering on their promises, predictable workflows continually strengthen. Conversely, when trust is lowered, doubt and friction flourish and workflows are impeded. As a leader, if you doubt that your team members will do what you have asked them to do or what they have promised, there are a few guarantees:

- **People will drift further away from each other.** They will keep to themselves, assume more, talk less, share less and listen less, and doubts and second guessing will spread to more areas of the workplace, burrowing deeper over time.

- **Doubt causes more work.** Leaders work harder to make up for the variances within the team. Doubts can creep into a leader's communication, creating more uncertainty in the minds of team members.

- **Doubt stops rhythm.** Rhythm is about knowing what is coming next. It is having complete and utter trust in the next step. As a leader, if you doubt your ability to perform, you will use vast sums of energy worrying and creating tension. If you doubt your team members will do their jobs well, then you will be distracted and start operating on all sorts of assumptions. If a team member doubts your communication or direction, they will also start operating on assumptions and worry about what will happen tomorrow.

Doubt cripples confidence, eroding trust in oneself and amongst the team. It happens slowly, gradually and quietly. Then, one day, all that erosion will result in a whole rock face being depleted. The team is dismantled, the value of its service diminished, and the business in real strife!

Whatever the context, leaders must have trust in themselves to breed trust in their teams. Trust is a big concept. Trusting yourself is an underlying leadership principle that builds a rhythmically performing team. In this book, we will delve into how you can build trust and rhythm in your team.

CHAPTER 3

The Real Game

"The less effort, the faster and more powerful you will be."
– Bruce Lee

Return On Effort (ROE) – The Team Performance Scale

If you were a professional sporting coach and the volume of training you put your athletes through had been maximised, what would you do?

This was the challenge facing elite international swimming coaches in the early '90s. The adage that the key to success is to increase the volume of training to gain better results (*the old paradigm*) was being questioned. Gennadi Touretski understood this when he coached Alexander Popov, the Russian short-distance swimming champion, as well as the Australian Swimming Team in 1992. It was a peculiar arrangement where Touretski, a man known for his scientific approach to coaching, was appointed the head of swimming at the Australian Institute of Sport, while Popov, a dedicated apostle of Touretski, paid his own expenses to train in Australia as a Russian national athlete.

During this time, Australia experienced a golden age of swimming, with greats like Kieren Perkins, Ian Thorpe and Michael Klim all becoming legends of Olympic swimming. At the same time, Popov dominated the 50-metre and 100-metre events by winning gold in both distances at back-to-back Olympics. Russian-born Touretski was a unique presence in swimming circles. His coaching methods were considered unorthodox and bizarre by many. He had swimmers dragged through the pool so they could get used to the feeling of swimming at a faster pace. He asked swimmers to hold their arms outside their cars while travelling at 90km/h so they could feel the resistance when their palm was open compared to when it knifed through the air.[18]

All Touretski's training boiled down to one principle: quality beats quantity. Efficiency of movement was his focus. As a degree-qualified engineer who majored in biomechanics, biochemistry, fluid mechanics and sports physiology, Touretski wanted his swimmers to glide through the water with as little resistance as possible.[19] To do this, they would have to forget everything the swimming world had thought was important. Throughout its history, the swimming world believed power was the aim of the game, but Touretski disagreed.

Up until this point, if you wanted to swim fast, you simply had to be the most powerful. The most powerful athletes were the ones who would come out on top. Touretski's new philosophy was obsessed with technique, which meant balance and a streamlined swimming action. This new way of swimming aimed to reduce stroke-rate to maximise energy consumption while increasing propulsion in the water (*the new paradigm*).

This philosophy understood that swimmers were not playing a game of speed; they were playing *a game of effort*. Underpinning this was the realisation that the effort swimmers put in during training and competition was finite, and had to be maximised to gain the best results possible. The equation of speed versus time didn't matter. What did matter was the *return on effort (ROE)*; the results that are achieved compared to output and exertion.

I believe this is the game we all play in our teams. ROE is the true leveller or truth teller of our professional lives. Leaders who understand this can leverage it, just like Touretski did when training his swimmers in the 1990s.

We all have a finite amount of time and resources to achieve our goals. And in reality, there are many ways in which we can get to the finish line.

ROE is the true leveller or truth teller of our professional lives. Leaders who understand this can leverage it.

But where is the actual finish line? In business, you could argue there is no finish line. When a salesperson achieves their sales for the month, another sales target awaits them the following month, then the following quarter, following half, following year, and so on. It is exhausting just thinking about it! So, maximising our energy expenditure, as Touretski's swimmers did, is super important.

Return On Effort

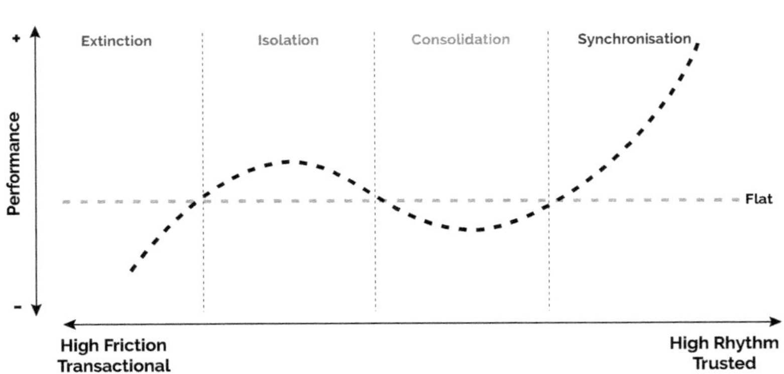

The *game of ROE* (see graphic above) is a windy one, where rhythm is our currency along the scale. It is not necessarily linear and has four distinct phases, all with contextual meaning and implications for our own journeys. The four phases are:

1. **Extinction.** Has little to zero rhythm. Everything seems jagged, has a lot of drag and the friction is intense. Basically, everything is hard work, and the harder we work, the worse things seem to get.

2. **Isolation.** Where some processes and people in our team have some form of flow, but it is stop-start and only happens occasionally or in some scenarios. Usually, results will be OK without being great, but because there is little rhythm, the results we get come at great expense and are unsustainable.

3. **Consolidation.** A phase of investment that turns isolated areas of flow into a widespread rhythm. It involves training, sharing, discussing, learning, listening and changing how we operate. Due to the nature of this phase, it is common (but not a certainty) for results to lower during this time, as people learn new ways of doing things, adapt to new philosophies and make mistakes while developing new skills.

4. **Synchronisation.** When the investments in consolidation pay off. Rhythm is seen throughout the team, and trust and respect are high, while engagement is through the roof. Processes, people and stakeholders are sync with each other. Company and team missions are also in sync with the daily behaviours of team members, and individuals are in sync with their workflows. It is a beautiful state of flow that repeats continuously, no matter what disruptions arise. Importantly, it is not propped up by ever-increasing working hours or more company/client resources.

ROE is a fluid model, where we can slip back and move forward at any given time. We can apply this to ourselves as individuals, and we can plot our team members and teams on this scale. We can even plot entire departments and organisations with the ROE model, but we will focus on ourselves as leaders and our teams. Once we understand that ROE is the game we are really playing, we can assert ourselves into a position where we make the decisions and take the actions that allow us to "glide" over the water rather than "fight" it.

Extinction Phase – An Absence of Team Rhythm

As discussed in Chapter 1, the current lifespan of a business is 17 years and getting shorter. We are seeing more large traditional businesses becoming extinct, resulting in major job losses and startled markets. Famous examples are Kodak, Blockbuster and Toys R Us. In January 2020, the Australian market saw 161 bricks-and-mortar retailers fail to remain open.[20] They went into administration and either became extinct or are on the brink of it. Long-term men's clothing store Ed Harry, sportswear giant Skins and department store Harris Scarfe are just some examples of well-known brands that have entered into various types of administration. These businesses were unable to remain viable during challenging economic conditions. And no matter where you are or what industry you are in, there are going to be challenging times.

Market commentary tells us that these businesses fell victim to lowered customer confidence and spending due to sluggish wage growth and an ever-increasing cost of living. This was made worse by the entry of global giants, such as H&M, Zara, Uniglo, Aldi and Sephora, which continue to attract larger chunks of customer spend and are squeezing out many local and well-established businesses, sending some multinational brands packing, too! Then there's the increased presence of online shopping and online specialists, such as The Iconic and Asos in the fashion marketplace, and the slowly increasing presence of Amazon and eBay on the retail landscape.

But are any of these factors a surprise? Did they happen overnight?

The answer is a resounding no. Internet shopping has been around for more than 20 years. Consumer spending has been fragile since I can remember, and American and European giants have been trying to enter the Australian market for decades. Many arrived rubbing their hands together, but went home with their tails between their legs as they did not understand the difficulties of the market. Some examples include Top Shop/Top Man, Hollister and Starbucks.* High wages, long distances and conservative shopping habits have always made Australia a tough place to flog your wares, and these businesses were to find that out.

Behind all these failed brands are people – leaders and professionals who are clever and experienced. But they were unable to implement actions to stop their businesses from becoming headline statistics. If

---

* Starbucks eventually re-entered the market for a second time with some success, but it was still limited compared to expectations. See: "Starbucks (Failure in Australian Market)." Business Studies Questions & Answers. (2017). http://www.businessstudiesqa. com/2017/12/starbucks-failure-in-australian-market.html

I were to be harsh on these people, I would say they were sleeping at the wheel. Old ways of working were not working, yet they ploughed on – eventually, to their demise. It is harsh, but the prospect of extinction is a glaring issue we all face in our respective playing fields.

If you are a professional sportsperson, you are only a few bad results away from being dropped from your team. If you are a fashion designer, you are only one bad season away from being flicked for another hot talent. If you are a TV producer, you are only one bad ratings season away from being fired. If we do get a second chance and are lucky to get a third, well, no one gets a fourth chance. None of us can escape this common truth. And it is this underlying reality that frightens us and ushers us towards self-preservation rather than progression. We simply work harder to hold on to what we have. We grip tighter, hoping things will turn around. I call this a *transactional style* of working. We shorten our lens to what is happening in front of our nose. We solve problems as they pop up, with little energy or time devoted to solving the systemic problems that will make the very same problems pop up again.

I see this often as a consumer. A gym I used to go to was like this. The exercise bikes were lined up facing the window adjacent to the front counter. I would hop on a bike, put my headphones on and peddle away for 20 minutes. During this time, I would watch the staff huddled around the computers, chatting or looking at their screens, or staring into space. Then a customer would approach them with a problem, and a staff member would try to sort it out. A queue would quickly form. As the staff member was unequipped to deal with the problem, they called over others to help. The queue gained momentum, becoming longer and impatient. Customers would get irritated, and the staff felt the pressure. They worked hard to clear the mess they had created for themselves. They apologised and hoped it would all be over soon.

Then, it was over. As quickly as the backlog came, it would be dead quiet again. The staff breathed, recovered and moaned about how hard that had been. Eventually, they got back to their natural state, but this time, they were tired, worn down and everything felt harder. The cycle was ready to be repeated, but with less fuel in the tank. While everyone else on the exercise bikes watched their screens, I watched this same pattern every day. The staff had no idea anyone was watching, but this is what I do. I am always watching staff and observing the moments that create a high or low ROE working environment, making the consumer experience either enjoyable or forgettable.

This transactional way of working is draining, demotivating and provides a horrible experience for everyone. No progress is possible, and zero rhythm is in play. A lot of resources are spent for little return. I would argue that it is this type of environment that leads to a business being fragile and brittle. It creates a survival culture that is not sustainable. The human body splutters over time due to stress, long hours and a sense of meaningless. Relationships break down as people don't feel cared for by their teammates or their boss, and they have to deal with unreliable processes. They become abrupt or uninterested with customers, and customers themselves switch off. They decide to go elsewhere, no matter what the price or marketing message says. These are the symptoms of being in the *extinction phase* of the ROE game.

The problem with being in the extinction phase is that it can be difficult to get out. A lot of effort and energy go into just remaining in the game. It's like a gambling addict borrowing from the house to stay at the table and win back their debts, except in most businesses, it is just as much about human energy and social reputation debt as it is about financial debt. There are only so many hours in the day, and there are only so many weeks you can put in 60 or 70-plus hours. Calling on favours from clients and suppliers can only be done so many times. At some stage, the candle will run out of wick.

We tend to find that the results we get in the extinction phase are poor or below one's *break-even point*. This can happen to any business or professional at any time. But if results are poor while a lot of resources are being used, this tells us we are in line for extinction.

The restraints of being in the extinction phase make things even harder. Poor results usually lead to cutbacks, which means there will be more to do with fewer resources, as saving money becomes the new mantra.

The biggest problem with this is that it makes us less intelligent. Our decision making becomes compromised. This was seen in a study of South American sugar cane farmers. A research team, led by Princeton University Professor Eldar Shafir, visited these farmers, who earnt the bulk of their money for the year in one hit – after harvest. This meant they were quite poor for most of the year until their big pay day. The research team tested the farmers' IQ before and after harvest. The results showed that the farmers increased their IQ scores by 13 points after the harvest. In other words, they were more intelligent when they had money in their pockets and did not have to worry about paying for shelter, food or transport. The study proved that the hardest thing about being poor is being poor itself. It compromises our problem-solving cognitive function.[21]

Shafir calls this a *scarcity mindset*, where a person becomes preoccupied with short-termism. They perform only the tasks in front of them well. This focus is strong, but it reduces the person's ability to think about things outside their immediate needs. Their lowered bandwidth creates forgetfulness and tardiness. In the context of a professional setting, this means critical thinking, problem solving, attention to detail and listening skills decline. When trapped in this mindset, our brains function like a computer running several large programs simultaneously. The computer will run slow, overheat, and, eventually, it may shut down.

If you are reading this and feeling a little uneasy, you are not alone. It is scary. But it is not an impossible situation to escape. In fact, the initial steps required to move out of the extinction phase are relatively simple and economical. By understanding that our survival instinct is the biggest driver of a transactional way of working, we can consciously shift our focus and the way we operate – as individuals, teams and organisations.

Self-preservation is a useful thing. It keeps us alive, safe and serves us well in many environments. But when the self is the sole focus, we create a negative spiral of performance. Some examples of *self-oriented* internal dialogue include:

- *"My department is more important than your department. We should be the priority. No one understands the urgency of our problems, and if only the rest of them stopped acting like lunatics, we would get what we need!"*

- *"I need to get that deal today. All I need to do is remember the wife's and kids' names, show them the original deal, and then give them the extra discount. I'll make it look like I'm doing them a favour, even though I have the go-ahead from my boss to discount as much as I need to – as long as it gets the deal over the line. If I get this done, I'll hit my target, which is all that matters right now."*

- *"The team needs to do better. They are making me look bad, and I'm not going to have it. All I do around here is clean up after them and do the work they miss. Not because I want to, but because I am the boss and I have to! I do the longest hours and no one thanks me. They don't care. They have no idea how much I do for them or how much I protect them from senior management. They need to start working harder. I'm not going to get it in the neck for them. I've had enough. I'll tell them the way it is from now on. They'll do it the way I say."*

This focus on self is so destructive and counterproductive that trust and rhythm are not possible. None of the above lines of thinking will result in good-quality work. None of them will create connection, inspiration or positive change. When we think of ourselves and our needs as the priority, the experience for all stakeholders tends to become *generalised*. Everyone becomes a number rather than a human. They are merely pawns in our game of chess. And, in return, we feel like a pawn in everyone else's game. When we feel like this, we see no real reason to engage. This disconnection means staff start searching Seek. com for other jobs. Clients start shopping around for alternatives. I have been in this situation myself as a manager. I felt disconnected from the brand and wanted to get out, yet I needed to fake my commitment and get my team to commit to the sinking ship. It was awful and, deep down, no one bought it.

When we become obsessed with saving our backside, there is an immediate lowering of trust in all relationships. As everyone is out for themselves, no one feels safe. No one has your back. Furthermore, an inward approach to our work can build feelings of anxiety, depression and confusion. A constant focus on our own problems escalates into a tsunami of destructive thoughts, which, once again, leads to poor decisions and saps our energy. It is for this reason that the initial step of getting out of the extinction phase is to STOP. Stop what you are doing and breathe. Please step away from your desk.

Look at the work that really needs to be done; not more mindless hustle and reactionary transactions so you can live for another day. The work is to ask some big questions and discuss the answers. In just one conversation, a strong and positive direction can be found; one where people feel included and clear on what they are meant to be doing. It may take a few conversations, depending on your context. But no matter the situation, as a leader, the discussion should focus on answering: *why are we all doing what we are doing?* The key is to ask yourself first before asking anyone else.

Some good examples of questions to ask yourself:

- *Why should my team bother to commit to this company (or to me)?*
- *Why would customers buy from us instead of our nearest competitor?*
- *Why does our day-to-day work matter?*
- *Why do I care? Why do I want to work here?*

I'll give you a hot tip. If your answer to any of these questions is money or a salary, it indicates you are operating in the old paradigm. When we have our backs to the wall and the pressure is on because results are tanking, we need to realign with the real reason our jobs exist. Without this alignment, money is not enough to make it worth it. There needs to be something more than money; otherwise, the fatigue of constant new targets wears us down, with no end in sight.

Some will find it difficult to answer the last question succinctly. But when the answer is unclear for the leader, it is probably a foundational reason why no one in the team cares about the work or product. No one is actively solving problems. Instead, the default is to deal with problems as they arise. By openly and honestly discussing this, with no agenda other than to make a better and more stable workplace, there is a good chance people will re-engage. It is a simple low-to-no-cost switch of mentality any leader can do, no matter how desperate the situation.

Simon Sinek became a world-wide phenomenon off the back of his first bestselling book, *Start With Why*. There is a reason it was such a hit. Answering the "why" question aligns our work with a meaningful purpose, and this, in turn, engages our team and customers. The transactional way of working simply cannot exist when our why is clear. People care too much. They are no longer just worried about themselves. They are concerned about the impact their work has on others and the bigger picture, and they want their contribution to make a difference.

Asking why is a simple and low-cost step, yet leaders of teams in the extinction phase feel they have zero time for such nonsense. Ironically, this very attitude results in them landing on the scrap heap.

Isolation Phase – Splats and Splutters of Team Rhythm

You know that feeling you get when things are just happening for you? Things come easily, and you feel light as a feather. You're *in the zone*. It's one of the best feelings on the planet!

I get this sometimes when I play golf. Occasionally, the club hits the ball sweetly. It sounds amazing! And the flight of the ball is straight and gentle, yet it penetrates the air. It is controlled, which is the best a hack golfer like me can hope for. Golf is a difficult game to play and do well in – especially when you don't practise, warm up before you play or play often. Yet when you experience those moments when everything works, it almost seems easy; dare I say, a little boring. This feeling of superiority washes over you, and you start to stand a little taller and smile a bit more. Then two holes later … Slice! Bunker! Water hazard! Four putt! If you know nothing about golf, you can assume these are all bad things. What makes them irritating is the fact that you were playing so good just a moment ago! Nothing has changed, yet the results have significantly fallen. It is frustrating and causes all sorts of tension.

This situation happens to us a lot in our work lives. We have moments of brilliance and excellence, but they are fleeting and, for some reason, only happen occasionally. We search for common ingredients in these moments, which leads us to create funny rituals, like having lucky underwear or carrying a lucky token in our pocket for a big project or important presentation. The reality is that none of these things makes a difference, other than to offer comfort and familiarity. In our workplaces, often our own performance is variable from day to day or task to task. Moments of brilliance may also come in a different guise…

- Maybe there is excellence in one section of our team, where one or two performers are brilliant at what they do, but everyone else struggles.

- Maybe one aspect of our team's work is done exceptionally well, but the rest is done inconsistently or is strewn with errors.

- Maybe some projects are completed on time, on budget and with a high level of quality, but most others lag and are interrupted by multiple pain points.

This inconsistency is common. In fact, in my experience, most of the marketplace finds itself in this scenario.

Here are some indicators that a team is suffering from inconsistency:

- A lot of good, hard-working people are doing their very best, and the result only just keeps the business afloat, above break-even point or just on (or around) planned targets.

- Just enough promotions or marketing campaigns are classified as successes to pull the business through from year to year.

- A brand has a hero product or product range that is responsible for the lion's share of revenue and is leveraged to prop results.

- A handful of key clients are heavily invested in the brand, with a big drop off in investment from all other clients.

In all these scenarios, the business is ticking along and results are being posted, but they are flimsy. They are propped up by the minority. Because of this, all stakeholders need to exert a lot of energy to get jobs over the line. With such an inconsistency in results and where they are coming from, a huge amount of effort is continually poured into the business's weak areas. With this comes frustration, cloudiness and confusion in a high-friction environment where ROE is usually low. There will almost certainly be lethargy, fatigue and low motivation.

What we are experiencing here is an over-reliance on isolated pillars of performance. All the ingredients are there to be "in flow" and gain rhythm. But without deep synchronisation, there is a stuttering. What is being done is not being repeated, particularly when so many proverbial eggs are in so few baskets. If your business is in this type of situation, then you are in the *isolation phase*. Good stuff is happening, which is important to acknowledge, but it is only happening sometimes or in a few areas. Not only does this mean people are working harder than they need to, but it also means the entire business is exposed to exterior forces of resistance. Operating in the isolation phase is more perilous than we think. We can be knocked into the extinction phase swiftly. This is why the *Star Model* has limited success.

From 1989–2001, a research team from Stanford University conducted one of the most in-depth studies of organisational cultures ever. Named the Stanford Project, staff practices of 200 tech start-ups were scrutinised to understand what model of team typology worked best. This meant the teams were recruited and operated based on five different cultural philosophies:[22]

1. **Star Model.** Find the best talent, pay them the best wages and give them all the resources they need to be their brilliant selves.

2. **Commitment Model.** Build a company people would never want to leave unless they were retiring.

3. **Bureaucratic Model.** Operate a business where nothing is left to chance. Everything is documented, procedures are tight, and everything is done with rigour and due process.

4. **Engineering Model.** Attract and keep people who enjoy the challenge of their work. Match skills to tasks and keep everyone in their lanes.

5. **Autocratic Model.** Do what you are told to do, get paid and go home. Hierarchy is respected above all. Rinse and repeat.

This study involved many intricacies, but a key result was each model's likelihood of failure. Firstly, the *Autocratic Model* performed very poorly and scored a very high percentage for the likelihood of failure. This links to the leadership styles we commonly see with teams in the extinction phase. The *Engineering Model* was next best with a neutral percentage, followed by the *Bureaucratic Model*, then the *Star Model*. The best-performing model was the *Commitment Model*. We will refer to this study again later in the book.

For now, I want to highlight the Star Model in relation to the isolation phase. This is where we may have some super-star performers, products, leaders or clients. It sounds great but creates high levels of risk.

What the Stanford Project showed was that a bunch of stars come with a lot of risk. They are high maintenance. They have big egos that need stroking. And sometimes, they simply do not perform. It is a flimsy way to do business. An over reliance on certain individuals or segments of the operation can lead to devastatingly precarious situations. Fighting for talent may not be worth the investment.

In the early 2000s, I worked for a beautiful cosmetics brand in the UK called Neal's Yard Remedies. It is famous for its blue bottles and organic herbal-based skin-care range. Year in, year out, sales were heavily reliant on the Frankincense Nourishing Cream. We sold tonnes of the stuff. This facial cream was a heritage product for the brand, and it wouldn't surprise me if it is still a top seller. One of the brand's outstanding points of difference was that the products were completely natural and organically certified. This was great, but it did mean the supply chain was fragile. Because the product was natural, there was a limit to how much the brand could stockpile. The brand's products were only one torrential downpour of rain (or bug infestation) away from going out of stock. Even if this never happened, there was an inherent fragility to the business. A standard had been formed where revenues and profits ticked along at an acceptable rate, so long as the hero product kept producing. If the unthinkable did happen, the brand would have slipped into the extinction phase immediately.

Is this happening in your team? Are you overly reliant on one part of your work to bring in results? Maybe as a leader, you are a charmer. Whenever you need to, you can put on that cheeky smile and persuade other departments, team members or clients to "do you a favour". Or maybe you are an excellent presenter, so you can always rely on producing a good pitch. Or perhaps you are a solid grinder; you keep your head down and go about your business with unrelenting reliability. No matter what your go-to trick is, overly relying on it can create a void beneath the thin veneer of your scoreboard results. A hint of doubt sits in the back of your mind. Knowing there is a lack of stability and depth in how we do business means every day is tinged with hesitation and wariness, and we hope that today is not the day when we'll be found out. This is a key inhibitor of being in rhythm.

As a leader, this tension and uncertainty take their toll. Usually, extra work must be done to cover the deficiencies. Nervous energy is continually burnt as we scramble through commercial gateways just to keep our results in the positive. The coaxing and extra effort it takes to keep the team on board and engaged from one period to another wear us down. It's a situation where good, hard-working people who are suddenly faced with any form of external event are automatically sent into the extinction phase. Maybe a new competitor enters the market or your star salesperson hands in their notice or a major client goes out of business. This is when things get desperate.

If you are not sure whether you or your organisation falls into this phase, observe whether the group's dialogue is obsessed with statistics. Is the conversation always about metrics – goals, targets, percentages, data or mix of business? These are critically important factors for anyone in any industry to talk about. But when they are obsessed about and focused on to the point of distraction from other vital areas, we lose focus on the bigger game and areas of performance that can help us build higher ROE. A good example of this is when a company is obsessed with being number one in their industry. It is fundamentally self-absorbed. Being number one is a great achievement, but if that is why you want everyone to work hard or your clients to buy from you, it is shallow and inward focused. It promotes protectionism rather than collaboration. A lot of our incentive schemes and company cultures rely on this mentality, and I believe it is the reason why most of the marketplace resides in the isolation phase.

The isolation phase is OK. Results are posted, and we are firmly entrenched in the game, which is a good thing. But it is fragile – more fragile than most are willing to admit. If we don't take invest in the right areas to spread those isolated pockets of brilliance to other areas, then it is only a matter of time before the veneer cracks, and we slip into extinction.

Having said that, the ingredients for finding flow and rhythm in our teams are there. With some cultivation, real rhythm can be grown with plenty of quick wins at hand to get the momentum up. The step from the isolation to consolidation phase is the performance step from the old paradigm to the new paradigm. The opportunity is in front of you. Your team and overall business desperately want to move into the new paradigm – they just need a leader to show them the way.

Consolidation Phase – The Step Towards Team Rhythm

As a leader, you may be asking what it is you can do to bring people together to synchronise. If you find that your team (or business) is surviving perennial extinction or that isolation is all too common for you, what can be done?

A good starting point is to realise that the friction and inconsistencies of being in this state are the result of irregularity. Work is being made harder by having to re-work problems or re-invent the wheel. You know when you attack your to-do list and find it has only grown by the end of the day? When your team members get in each other's way? When you moan about clients rather than enjoy working with them? These are all classic symptoms of a team working without rhythm, where members lack synchronisation with each other and the marketplace.

When we are in this situation, we know something needs to change. And the leader needs to make a confession. Admitting to yourself that things must change and that you probably need to change how you work and make decisions is the most powerful first step. As mentioned previously, this is where the hard work lies. The leader and team members need to set their egos aside. Initially, this is scary and confronting, but it becomes incredibly liberating. Since understanding this for myself, I find I am at my best when I admit to what I have been doing wrong (or poorly). Each day, I ask myself how I could improve my way of doing things. This is not to be constantly critical of myself, but to detach from how I do things rather than be defensive. As Don Miguel Ruiz states in his book, *The Four Agreements*: *"Personal importance, or taking things personally, is the maximum expression of selfishness because we make the assumption that everything is about me."* Ruiz adds, *"We think we are responsible for everything. Me, me, me, always me!"*[23]

This self-consumed line of thinking draws our teams back towards the extinction phase and causes a lot of friction in the work environment. By throwing off the shackles of making everything about us, by being open to new ways of thinking and working, we can begin to piece together the ingredients to create our own flow and cycles of rhythm. We can start to experience more creativity for ourselves and our teams. It is a great first step. But this, in itself, will not move our teams out of isolation. A larger body of work is required.

We may need to go slow to go fast. We may need to invest when we feel we need to cut back. We may need to bring people closer when there's little trust and respect. Central to making any of this happen is shifting our focus away from our needs and the numbers. The results need to take a backseat. We need to be ready to shield our team from the onslaught of pressure that may rain down on us as we shift our focus away from outcomes to the only thing that will create forward momentum: our people.

Richard Branson is famous for saying, *"Clients do not come first. Employees come first. If you take care of your employees, they will take care of the clients."* This is a fundamental principle of business, and I could not agree more. Yet friction will continually pull our focus away from our people. This means high performers get zero attention and poor performers receive begrudged attention that is ineffective at best. We tend to invest in platforms and tech tools with vigour, but the volume of spend on professional development in most companies is minimal to non-existent. John Seely Brown, researcher and author of *The Social Life of Information*,[24] says companies invest 95% of their spending on business processes, with only 5% going towards supporting ways to mine a corporation's *human capital*. He states, *"The tangibles of processes overrule the intangibles of people."* And I can easily see why we do this.

Processes are under our complete control. They do what we tell them to do. They are the property of the business and will be in our business until we decide to get rid of them. Processes and tools are straightforward; they either work or they don't. They are easy to measure and manage. Hence, the term tangible. People, on the other hand, are dynamic, prone to all sorts of risk. For starters, they can leave the company. They can let us down no matter what we do to support them. In fact, even the best employees will probably let us down at some point. So, why would we invest in them? With the little resources we have, how can we spare expenditure on people who will inevitably leave or disappoint?

It is a depressing and bleak perspective. Yet, it is reality, and to not acknowledge this is to live in a fairy tale. But if we can find another perspective, we may be able to make progress. What would happen if we could invest in our people as if they were a process? What would this look like and would it work?

When faced with such questions, I put my facilitator's hat on to find gaps in the problem. Let's flip the argument by being devastatingly practical:

What would happen if we did not invest in our people?

We know that the isolated good stuff happening in our teams would become worn out, fatigued, unmotivated and, at some stage, undone. We know the exhaustion of continually trying to survive will seal our fate, and we will become extinct sooner or later. We know that behind every tool, platform, process and protocol in our workplace is a human using it. If humans don't use these "tangible tools" consistently well, then they are quite useless to us. We know that if we lose our best people and performance manage our worst people, we will need to continually recruit, which is expensive and time consuming with little chance of getting better results.

Instinctively or intellectually, we know all this. So, it is up to us as leaders to put our big-boy or big-girl pants on and take a stand. We need to bite the big one and get honest quickly and work closer with our team. We need to get everyone's heads together and start a new dawn where we work differently. It can be the ignition of a new journey or adventure. And the best bit is we can start now. Today. There is no need to wait for the next meeting, the beginning of the new quarter or a fancy off-site retreat. It can all start right now, just by making the decision. And decisions are wonderful things. The act of making a decision is the act of cutting out all the other things we could do (the origin of the word "decision" is to *cut off*). If I were to remain in facilitator mode, I would then ask:

How will we activate this new decision to consolidate the team and form a robust unit that creates a cumulative higher ROE for every stakeholder?

A natural starting point is to figure out what is working and what is not. Because of our continual busyness, we probably already know what these things are, but have not acted on or explored them. So, get a blank piece of paper and draw a line down the middle. On the left-hand side of the page, title the column *Awesome Stuff.* Write down the parts of the business or your direct team that are performing brilliantly consistently. They look great, yield great results and require little attention or resources. Then, on the right-hand side, title the column *Awful Stuff.* Now, this could be truly uncomfortable, but remember, this exercise is based on brutal honesty and positive intention. We may need to write down people's names or things we do ourselves. That's OK. At this stage, there is no need to share your list. It is an exercise to find clarity for yourself so you can make strong, considered decisions.

Have you done it? If you haven't, then stop reading! I don't care if you are on the train or in bed. I'm going to be annoying now – please stop reading and write down those five or 10 awesome/awful things you instinctively know about your business and team. It will only take a minute but could save careers and even your entire business. If you think that is overly dramatic or simplistic, I can testify to witnessing years of unnecessary pain because intelligent, hard-working folk didn't take a moment to consolidate their thoughts and observations. It makes a significant difference.

The *consolidation phase* is related to a lowering in revenue or KPI results. The reason for this is because a leader needs to invest time, energy and money into their people's development and change how things are done. It is a time of learning. And learning costs. It also yields great outcomes (sometimes), but primarily costs. The reason for this is that people will need to change how they work, which is difficult for most. Change is scary, and anything scary flicks on our flight/fright/freeze mechanism, which does not serve us well in the journey we are undertaking. We also need to teach our people new concepts, skills and ways of thinking. This takes a lot of mental energy and time for you and your team. It draws focus away from daily work, clients and the things that have been helping us scrape over the line.

There is also the inevitability that more mistakes will be made. As people try new things and start implementing new ways of working, they will slip up. Think back to when you learned how to ride a bike and all the grazes you got from falling over. Eventually, though, you got the hang of it, and it became easy. That is the same process our people need to go through. There will be grazes, tears and dummy spits.

Scott Belsky is an American entrepreneur famous for authoring *The Messy Middle*, in which he educates us on human happiness throughout our life cycle. His research suggests there is a U-curve of happiness, where we tend to be the most unhappy in the middle of our lives. Belsky states, *"Progress looks messy in the middle."* And, for our teams, this step into consolidation will look and feel messy, but it is the process we must go through when learning and developing. If we hold onto our old ways of working and thinking, ironically, our ROE will erode and eventually fall off the cliff. But if we hold the mistakes loosely, communicate closely and acknowledge the small signs of progress, we will start to experience that beautiful feeling of momentum and begin to leverage the new paradigm of rhythm.

Some practical first steps to lead your team into the consolidation phase:

- **Start small.** List the Awesome Stuff. Highlight the people who are doing a seemingly small skill brilliantly and get them to share how they do it with everyone else. Follow this up with individuals to support their implementation and stick with it for at least a month until everyone is crushing it. A great quick win.

- **Audit and hunt.** Take your list of Awesome Stuff and Awful Stuff and use it as a skills audit. What are the most significant impact areas that need attention? Start hunting for solutions. This may be in the form of courses, buddy systems or learning programs for specific individuals to develop them in the areas that need bolstering.

- **The cost of inaction.** If there is no budget to invest in consolidating your team, review the business to understand the cost of inaction. What would happen if the brilliant team member left? If the critical account went to a competitor? If you got sick? If a key process broke down? Start talking with leadership about cost. It is a language everyone understands. Suddenly, the investment budget for reducing such risks will become a lot easier to justify.

- **Become obsessed with staff.** As a leader, spend the majority of your time thinking about, supporting and injecting energy and resources into staff. Use data, but only in a way that helps you get clear on what staff needs to be their best. You, your clients and the "higher ups" can take a back seat in terms of importance. Become obsessed with your people and what they need to become rock stars.

I do not doubt that the decision to graduate into the consolidation phase is the most critical. It is the step that turns good, hard work into great flow, and is the defining act that results in leaders standing tall and respected in 10 years' time (the ultimate goal for us as leaders when utilising rhythm as a performance concept). It sets up a legacy and creates a cultural ripple felt long after we have moved on.

Synchronisation Phase – Pure Team Rhythm is the Norm

I don't like talking about "the best" very much. When we think of the best leaders in history or the best sporting teams or the best anything, it can be a fun discussion, but how helpful is it to us mere mortals? If we are talking leadership, stories of Abraham Lincoln, Alexander the Great, Mahatma Gandhi and Steve Jobs tend to dominate. These can provide us with the odd lesson and occasional dash of inspiration, but often, we can't help but compare ourselves to them. We think, *"I could never change the world like they did,"* or, *"I could never be a great leader like them."* And that is a rational thought for many of us to have. These people did extraordinary things and changed the world they lived in dramatically. The odds are that many of us will not have such an impact. This can make us feel defeated before we start. There is nothing terrible about talking about "the best", but I question what it changes for us. Instead, I like to discuss "being better". Better is attainable, accessible and aspirational for all.

Can I be a better leader? Can we be a better team? Can our clients be better partners? Can we synchronise better?

Absolutely!

Synchronisation is a term many of us know. We have a sense of what it means, but there is very little literature, study or historical documentation on it, much like rhythm. When researching the keys to rhythm, I discovered that the ability to sync with each other and our environment is central to the process of creating rhythm in our teams. But when I bunkered down to research what I could find on this mysterious concept, what I found was a little disappointing. There was a lot of information about syncing devices and software systems and using the cloud. Then there was the philosophy of synchronicity – an esoteric and spiritual relationship, usually with a cosmic twist. None of this was insightful in my pursuit of this practical body of work focused on leading high-performing teams.

The *synchronisation phase* represents a way of working where everyone is aligned, everyone is in sync with each other, and a lot of work is getting done very easily. The flow state is experienced most of the time, and trust levels between team members are through the roof. Instead of everyone focusing on themselves, the team's mindset has grown into one based entirely on service. People are serving their manager, clients, peers and community. With all this service, there is no time to think about one's own problems. Team members are completing each other to form a unit rather than *competing* with one another. The skill level of the team is high and relevant to the work that needs to be done. This is thanks to the investment of time and energy in the consolidation phase, where best practices were shared, developed and perfected. There is a deep connection between all stakeholders, who are in it together to do meaningful work. Finally, for all this to come together, the magic of timing is essential.

According to W. Timothy Gallwey, author of *The Inner Game of Golf* (and the entire Inner Game series of books), the golf swing is the most complex action of all sport. Hundreds of individual movements need to be executed by almost every muscle in the body in a sequence that must be near-on perfect for the ball to be struck, so it goes in the intended direction and the intended distance. All this must happen in a split second. It is a wonder anyone can hit a golf ball well at all!

Our teams are the same. We may have five or 10 team members, all of whom have multiple task lists that change daily, maybe even hourly. They may have teams operating below them, too. All these people need to continually adapt and flex to all sorts of environmental shifts, stakeholder requests and new information. Just like the golfer who must adjust their foot position on uneven turf or move their aim slightly to accommodate a gust of wind, our teams make unique modifications all the time. As leaders, we must coordinate an array of variables, so everyone synchronises in order for the team to produce a metaphorical symphony equivalent to the Vienna Philharmonic Orchestra performing a rousing rendition of a Johann Strauss classic.

To achieve synchronicity is challenging but attainable for us all. And we do not need the biggest budgets, the best talent in the marketplace or the latest technology. Far from it, as the dabbawalas of India show us. Famous for being studied by Harvard University, the dabbawalas are a group of semi-literate men who deliver lunches from homes to workers six days a week, every week, throughout Mumbai, India. Since 1890, this institution has survived famines, wars, monsoons, riots and terrorist attacks. The dabbawalas deliver dabbas (metal lunch tins) from the homes to the desks of more than 130,000 workers every day.[25] It is not only a logistical marvel, but it is also a beautiful service that connects workers with their families and homes. Generally, wives or mothers prepare a home-cooked meal, package it, and have it ready for the dabbawala to collect. Then, within a few hours, it will be at the intended destination. Workers enjoy a freshly cooked meal from their loved ones, reinforcing a sense of connection and love. Then, just as swiftly, the tins are picked up after lunch and returned to each person's home.

This service is integral to daily life in Mumbai due to many reasons:

- Eating out is considered expensive.
- Cramped commuter trains mean taking a lunchbox to work is near impossible.
- Offices are generally absent of cafeterias.
- There is a cultural preference for home-cooked meals.

To appreciate this amazing feat, we must understand what a dabbawala's day looks like. These men, in all-white uniforms (including their signature white hats), ride their bikes to a cluster of houses to make their pick-ups. Then, they gather at the nearest train station, where the dabbas are sorted into crates according to destination. Each dabbawala takes their allocated crate of lunches onto the train, which takes them to the train station closest to their destination. The dabbas are sorted again by specific address so that the dabbawalas can deliver the lunches to specific offices, floors and desks. After lunch, the reverse is done to get the dabbas back to their rightful homes. It is a fine example of the synchronisation of thousands of moving parts. This living, breathing mechanism involves approximately 200 units (teams) of staff, each with about 25 people, operating with autonomy and devastating reliability.

Many rival services have come and gone, but none has been able to match the service and value for money the dabbawalas have provided for more than 100 years. The dabbawalas are an excellent example of what is possible. Harvard University has used this case study in management articles, techniques and courses. The four highlighted lessons are:

1. **Organisation.** A high-standard procedure where high-level execution is imperative. The one non-negotiable is that everyone

sticks to the plan and does their job on time and with complete accuracy.

2. **A flat hierarchy.** This is a trend in our Western organisations, although maybe not to the extent of the dabbawalas. It is best described by Professor Stefan Thomke as a *"self-organised democracy"*. There is management but, overall, it works because members of the group self-police each other and keep each other accountable.

3. **A belonging culture.** A deep emotional bond exists between the teams. They proudly share an identity and a camaraderie. Their mission is simple: *deliver food on time, every time.* And every single one of them buys into this wholeheartedly.

4. **Systems that stack.** From the simple coding system chalked onto every dabba to the way the train system is used and the use of bicycles. Every system stacks on top of each other. Change to one system impacts all others – something many Western businesses continually fail to understand.**

I feel that efficiency, effectiveness and productivity represent the promised land many leaders search for. But I propose that these are merely stepping stones towards the real gold: *synchronisation*. When we are all in sync, we are all engaged. We can execute top-quality work with less effort, and we can enjoy the experience individually and as a group. There are minimal jagged edges or pithy political snides rumbling below the surface. But it is not perfect. There are still problems and mistakes, and there will always be exterior forces creating hardships.

But the team in synchronisation is equipped and ready to deal with these challenges positively, swiftly and with minimal disruption.

** Technology and motorbikes have been trialled by the dabbawalas and competitor organisations, but none of them worked because they did not stack with the other systems – most notably, the Mumbai train network. This proves that the latest, slickest technology is not always the best way to go. Syncing tech, processes and people is much more important than getting the newest, flashiest standalone tech tool – a temptation all too many modern businesses fall for.

It is an exciting aspiration, and I invite you to explore the world of rhythm and synchronisation for yourself. Like a church choir, your team can sing in pure harmony. And studies tell us that people in choirs experience amazing psychological and physiological positives. Their mental wellbeing improves, resulting in higher levels of resilience. A stronger feeling of togetherness is experienced, which feeds that sense of belonging all humans crave.[26] In fact, participants in one study reported reduced stress and depression levels, mainly due to an increase in oxytocin, which helps control stress and anxiety responses.[27]

The act of synchronising with other people in a team is powerful. It sets the team up with all the capabilities of rhythm, so loops of improvement, feedback and execution can continue. It is beautiful. And if we can lead our people to operate like this, we can touch many lives positively and constructively. This is the power of the Rhythm Effect, and it can amplify well beyond your team into your wider community. As leaders, it is a tool that lifts our profile and influence, as we are the ones who set the tone and are in the perfect position to start the process, one action at a time.

CHAPTER 4

The Leader's Journey

*"There has never been so much innovation in the world,
yet there has been a lack of progress where progress
means people's lives are better."*
– Anand Giridharadas, Winners Take All

Where does a leader sit within all this rhythm, synchronisation and ROE stuff?

I find it helpful to look at leadership from the point of view of the ROE scale. When a team is in the extinction phase, the leader is most probably leading from a similar position. This is reflected in the six phases of the leader's journey, which we will explore in this chapter. You can see this journey as a ladder, with the last step (*the progressor*) being a leader who achieves ongoing rhythm in their workflow and that of their team. Synchronisation flows through all their operations, and the ripple effects of this are powerful and felt by all – sometimes industry wide.

Leadership is a huge subject. In terms of learning rhythm, it is important to identify your leadership style within the leader's journey framework and plot your way through the journey, from survivor to progressor. This is a great way to understand your position and reflect on what you are experiencing, highlighting opportunities to enhance your performance and sync your team more and more.

We cannot afford
to hope or wait for
born leaders to come
along.

Leaders – Are They Born? What is Their Purpose?

Throughout my life, I have witnessed more terrible leaders than good ones. I have been a terrible leader myself at times. And many people considered to be great leaders have said and done terrible things in terms of leadership. Take Winston Churchill, for example. Hailed as one of history's best political leaders, he showed tremendous resilience and stubbornness to impact a favourable outcome against the Nazis in World War II. Yet he was also the architect of one of the biggest military gaffs in World War I, resulting in the decimation of Australian, New Zealand and Allied forces on the shores of Gallipoli, Turkey.[28] Churchill would rise back into a position of political power and be recognised as a leader who changed the world. Was he born a great leader and unlucky in WWI? Was he a terrible leader who got lucky in WWII? Or did he develop into a better leader? Or is it a combination of both? Maybe it is none of the above.

Streams of literature argue for all sides of the above debate. In my experience, we cannot afford to hope or wait for born leaders to come along. Teams that display high levels of synchronisation have many leaders amongst their ranks. And whether we like it or not, leadership is bestowed on us consistently and at inopportune moments – from speaking up at a community gathering, to helping an elderly person get their shopping to their car, to helping a team in another department deliver a project. These leadership moments and roles constantly come at us. Many of us shy away from these opportunities. Many of us fail to recognise them or understand what the situation requires so we can lead proficiently.

I believe we are born with natural talents and are deeply influenced by our environments. Motivational speaker Jim Rohn is attributed with the classic line, *"We are the average of the five people we spend the most time with."* This flies in the face of the *born to lead* theory, used to explain historical figures like Alexander The Great. "Born to lead" makes no sense to me. It would mean that if we do not achieve anything significant by the time we are teenagers or in our 20s, we are thrown onto the leadership scrap heap. We then become grunts destined to follow. As life-long non-leaders, we witness leaders screw things up with poor communication skills and decision making. We resentfully snide and moan, becoming desolate and disinterested in anything to do with work. Because we can only ever be an underling, we find ourselves in a hopeless situation. We have no agency and no ability to take the lead.

I believe we all have agency and can lead with every interaction we have. Even in small ways, we can lead and guide ourselves and others towards better experiences and outcomes. It is something all of us can develop, and to go back to Rohn's point, if we are surrounded by wise teachers and leadership mentors, we will learn what it takes to be a great leader. At that point, it is up to us to find our own way and style.

We all need to hone our abilities to take charge and lead others. We will make errors along the way and experience self-doubt at times. But over time, our leadership responsibilities grow, and with every step up, we revert to feeling like the new kid at school, uncertain of what will come next. We may feel intimidated by the challenges ahead, wondering if people will listen to us and fall in line. It is a tough gig. But someone's got to do it, and it might as well be you. So, let's crack on and work through a useful scale of leadership that helps us understand our journey of development.

To be a good leader, we need to understand what a leader does. It is difficult to pinpoint, and while studying the subject over the past decade, I have been in the gallery, observing opinions and assertions on the subject from all walks of life. As an avid sports follower, I watch and listen to a lot of sports commentary and discussion. Sport has become a public and easily accessible forum to understand teamwork, leadership and all sorts of topics that relate to our working life. Yet, ex-players, coaches and professional sporting greats often speak of leadership in narrow, poorly defined terms. I often hear that captains need to be the toughest players and stand up in big moments – to grab the game by the scruff of the neck! They are meant to be miraculous demi-gods who perform extra hard at pivotal moments, on top of how hard they are already meant to perform. They are expected to conduct charming interviews and influence the wider community whenever they are on camera. And, of course, they need to win!

Winning is what it is all about. A great leader wins. In our workplaces, that means they bring in the results. They keep to budgets and they hit the KPIs. Winners are grinners, after all.

I find these expectations of leaders a little outdated. That is, if they were ever the truth in the first place. I find this attachment to results and being the "best of the best" to be not only misguided when it comes to leading high-performing teams, but also destructive – to people and to the very results they want to achieve. As Simon Sinek poses in *The Infinite Game*, how can winning be the objective when the game we are playing does not have a defined end? Unlike a football match, we don't have a starting whistle, game clock or final whistle (or siren, depending on the type of football!).

Once a financial period is completed, another begins. The idea that success is hitting a target at the end of a period is limited in its helpfulness, especially when we are immediately rewarded with another bigger-and-tougher-to-achieve target for the next period. Often, we get this target with fewer resources and more pressure – cue stress!

I would argue that the same is true in the sporting world. Let's say you lead your team to the championship or premiership. Then what? Win another one? And another? It is an unforgiving pattern that can render the whole challenge meaningless. One mantra that makes me laugh is that of Australian rules football clubs, which generally all have a mission that includes the line: *"We exist to win premierships."* This is meant to inspire a culture of high standards and excellence, but when almost every club has the same mantra, it falls short of any real meaning. Winning is important for all our workplaces, but it is not everything, and it is not the sole purpose of a leader – far from it!

When we broaden our approach to leadership, we can practically and meaningfully apply ourselves to a cause, one that every stakeholder is happy to put their time, effort and energy into. Having a clear and well-rounded purpose gives a leader vigour, lightness and enthusiasm; a freshness they can inject into their team. What if the goal was simply to progress our situation? There would be a well-defined mission and milestones to achieve. And by pulling people together to create real progress for our company and, most importantly, our customers (and community), we can tap into a well of dynamic and exciting possibilities.

Another way to look at this is to see what happens when progress is not made. Take our current infatuation with our best friend, the smartphone. Mobile phones have helped us communicate with each other in increasingly intimate ways, from talking to people no matter where they are, to sending them messages, to sharing pictures and videos. We live in a time when most of us carry around a mini computer with more operating power than the tech used on the Apollo 11 spaceship.[29] The way smartphones have transformed our lives is astronomical. Yet how much progress has our society made since their introduction?

Smartphones cause all sorts of medical conditions that didn't happen or even exist before they came along. Children have shorter attention spans, new depression and anxiety conditions are prevalent, and even the ways we think and relate to each other have changed. Yet we are still just as stressed and working just as long hours as ever before.[30] As much as I cannot imagine a world without smartphones, I acknowledge that they have not necessarily progressed our society's happiness, equity or harmony. And it is this lack of progress we must be aware of as leaders. If progress is not being made under our direction, then what is the point? Why would anyone stick at their job? And why would anyone follow you?

Once we realise the purpose of leadership is to progress a given situation, we can get on with becoming what I call *the progressor* – a leader (and the last step of the leader's journey) who can harness a group of people into a *rhythmic progress machine*. The journey towards becoming a progressor is a long and eventful one. It is an adventure we can choose to take, but sometimes the adventure chooses us. It isn't easy, but I promise, it is fulfilling and, if you play, you cannot lose – as long as your intention is to create progress.

The All Blacks rugby team follows the mantra, *"Leave the jersey in a better place."* As leaders, our job is to leave our post and team in a better place than we found them. Everything else is a distraction.

There are six stages in the leader's journey:

1. **Survivors**
2. **Existors**
3. **Followers**
4. **Motivators**
5. **Attractors**
6. **Progressors**

Six Stages of the Leader's Journey

	Stage	Style	Rhythm
Infinite	PROGRESSOR	Trusted	
	ATTRACTOR	Respected	
	MOTIVATOR	Engaged	
Finite	FOLLOWER	Reliable	
	EXISTOR	Agreeable	
	SURVIVOR	Transactional	

Let's explore these leadership stages in detail.

Survivors – Transactional Leadership

"Survival mode" is a term commonly used for when we hit tough times and need to dig in to get through the pain. For example, when a farmer needs to cut all expenditure to get through a drought or when a ship's crew has to batten down the hatches to get through a storm. We all have a version of this, and at any given time, we can be forced back into this way of working.

Signals we are in the *survivor* leadership stage include:

- Focusing on short-term solutions
- Making quick decisions with little discussion
- Prioritising urgency over importance
- Considering bare-minimum service levels as sufficient
- Cutting back on perceived luxuries
- Stepping in to complete the team's tasks

When one or a combination of the above occurs within leadership, the rest of the team will likely follow. We can become judgmental of this kind of behaviour, as we know it involves compromise and will not yield progress. Yet when we acknowledge that survival mode is part of life and that none of us will go through sustained periods without needing to operate within it, we can shrug off any shame associated with it.

Some of my favourite times in my career were when I was forced into survival mode. When I was a retail manager, retail staff sometimes called in sick on the busiest day of the week, and I had to get "back on the tools" and rally the troops through an exhausting day. It was a shared experience where everyone felt the pain and helped out. At the end of it, everyone turned around and said, *"Paul, can we not go through that again?!"* But the beers we shared at the end of days like that were some of the best-tasting drinks we'd ever had.

In IT circles, times like these are called *crunch time* (as discussed in Chapter 2). They can be exciting, adrenaline-fuelled times. When the team gets through whatever they need to get through, the sense of shared achievement creates a real buzz. The problem is when crunch time becomes the norm. The human body cannot sustain being in perpetual survival mode. Teams fatigue, motivation drops and leaders become drained and disillusioned.

When survival mode becomes the norm, we set up a transactional leadership style and culture. Everything is an individual exchange, and there is no systemic progress or change. It is fatiguing, boring and costly on many levels. In my experience, leaders adopt this style more than we would like to admit. Our ego cannot hack the admission that we are working hard but not smart; that we are failing to be the amazing leader we hoped to be.

Acknowledging that a transactional style is our *modus operandi* is a critical step. Knowing it is not the answer to creating a more effective team is all we need to do to pull ourselves out of this desperately difficult situation. When we acknowledge that we are "in the shit" and need to survive, we can set our people up to get through the tough times to the point of safety. Goals are set around that point of safety so everyone can take stock and turn their attention to more systemic solutions. Once this change in mindset occurs, everyone can put their heads together to figure out what needs to be done to set up more sustainable ways of working, where longstanding problems are solved, and a culture of progress is generated.

Existors – Agreeable Leadership

Survivor leaders tend to give their all, which should be commended. They work exceptionally hard, and often carry the burden for the team or entire organisation. It's not clever or sustainable, but they are trying their hardest to keep the lights on and push through with minimal fuss. They are generally more admirable than existor leaders.

Existors are leaders who do not stand out. That is their superpower. They are grey, exist in the shadows and do not cause disruption. It doesn't sound so bad, but default existorship is. It can be highly dangerous for organisations to have existors in the business, let alone in leadership positions. When people have been in a job for too long or are simply in the wrong role, they lack engagement and passion. It can happen to the best of us. And we are kidding ourselves if we don't think this type of person resides in our teams.

Existors are often quite likable. If they are not likable, they are at least unnoticeable. They do not cause resistance or friction with big blow ups or dramatic boardroom scenes. They do not question or pose alternative points of view, and they are rarely contrarian in any way. Existors undermine team performance through 1,000 paper cuts.

Because of boredom or a desire hold on to comfort, existors will agree with whatever their seniors say. They may even agree with statements and poor decisions from peers and junior staff. They don't build a case or engage with a problem; they just want to punch the clock, get their paycheque and go home. Sometimes, agreeing to do a little more work is preferable to having to argue or stand up to injustices or poor decisions. It is easy to see why existors are not respected.

Now, don't get me wrong – sometimes, the best thing a leader can do is fall in line, be quiet or let sleeping dogs lie. This can be a shrewd and strategic move. But when this agreeable style is the established way of working, people do not feel protected, inspired or motivated. Trust diminishes. The signal is that nothing is worth fighting for and caring is unimportant.

Traits of existor leadership include:

- **Yes sir.** Too much yes and not enough no. Prioritising likability and popularity over performance not only compromises vision and results, but it also lowers trust. As social psychologist Susan Newman writes in *The Book of No*, *"We live under this misconception that saying yes, being available, always at the ready for other people, makes us a better person, but in fact it does quite the opposite. You get stressed and anxious; you're viewed as a patsy."*[31]

- **Too nice.** Being nice and playing by the rules is a real turn off. A research group asked subjects to play a game with individual and group rewards, and tracked their reactions to selfish moves and generous moves. The study found that people disliked the generous moves the most; they made them feel bad about themselves. They also felt that the people who played generous moves did not fit in with the social norm of the group (i.e. they were undermining the fun of the game and made others feel guilty about their own moves).[32] Being overly agreeable can lose us respect in our work circles, even if it comes from a virtuous and nice place.

- **Social harmony.** There is a phenomenon called *groupthink*. This is when everyone in a team thinks the same way and independent thought is not valued. There is a lack of ideas, and the first obvious solutions are agreed upon. Fundamentally, existors prioritise social harmony over innovation and performance. They disregard the importance of diversity in teams – not only demographically, but psychologically.[33] Leaders who do not encourage people to disagree promote groupthink.

Existor leadership creates drag and mediocre performance. Engage in this leadership style, and it won't be long before projects and entire operations slip into survival mode. In fact, existor leadership is the roadblock to getting out of the extinction phase and entering the isolation phase.

Existors tend to have a *protectionist mindset* that is mostly driven by fear. When fear is the motivation, there will always be doubt, rendering any form of personal rhythm, let alone team rhythm and synchronisation, impossible. Asking existors what it is they want and questioning the path they are taking will help them spring out of any slump or stupor. Exploring what stops us from engaging deeply with the problems we are meant to solve and the people we are meant to serve is a quick, low-to-no-cost activity that will take us out of this mode and move us forward in our leadership journey.

Followers – Reliable Leadership

When I was in my early 20s, I got my first managerial role in Cambridge, UK. I was a cricketer who worked in retail part time for extra beer money. As a fully qualified naturopath, I wanted to use my knowledge in retail when the cricket season finished. So, I applied for a supervisor's role advertised in the smaller of the two Holland & Barrett stores in town (the biggest corporate health foods retailer in Europe at the time). After one interview, I was hired as the assistant manager of the bigger store! Intensifying the situation was the absence of a manager for that location. On top of this, I found out it was the second-biggest store in the whole East Anglia region, and one of the biggest in the country!

All of a sudden, I found myself well and truly out of my depth. Later, I would realise this situation had all the hallmarks of an organisation that had issues. But at the time, I had no option but to follow. By following, I was able to lead the team to some sort of order and stability. I had to learn the processes. I had to take cues about prioritisation, team organisation and company cultures from my area manager and the managers from surrounding stores. When I look back, I wish I had called my peers more often with the mountain of questions I had every day. I built a good relationship with the manager at the bigger store in Ipswich, who helped me immensely. It was one of the smartest moves I could have made, even though all I was doing was trying to survive!

I went through the initial stages of survival mode. I was dealing with a team of mini existors but did not have the time or opportunity to fall into existor leadership. I jumped straight into *follower* leadership. And followership turns out to be a critical part of leadership.

The ability to follow is a useful way of leading. My time at Holland & Barrett is a prime example of when following is the best thing a leader, especially one who is new to a leadership role or business, can do. Every leader, no matter how high they are in the hierarchy, has someone to report to. Everyone must follow someone else. So, what does good followership look like from a leadership perspective?

Robert Kelley, a professor at the Graduate School of Industrial Administration at Carnegie Mellon University, has studied followership in detail. He has discovered the key traits of a good follower:[34]

1. **They take direction and execute.** Others can delegate to them, and they can self-manage their own process without needing systemic supervision. They follow instructions and honour the authority of others, while simultaneously carrying out instructions without needing their hand to be held.

2. **They see themselves in line with their boss.** Good followers do not consider themselves inferior and are not intimidated by people higher in hierarchies. In fact, they don't pay much attention to hierarchies. They understand that everyone has a job, and no one is more important than anyone else. They question their leaders to make sure they have a good understanding of initiatives, and partner with their boss rather than be sub-servant to them.

3. **They see the bigger picture.** Good followers can see that everyone above, below and sideways to them has their own goals and directives. Knowing that everyone has their own pressures and milestones to hit allows followers to see how their work fits in with everyone else's, giving them an understanding and interest in the company's broader goals, vision and mission.

Followers are reliable in every sense of the word. When I look back at that first managerial gig of mine, I can see that reliability was at the forefront of my intention, even if I didn't realise it at the time. I needed to turn up on time, follow procedures carefully and do what I said I would do so that the team would develop confidence in me and buy into their work. I had to be reliable to get through my probation period. I had to show my area manager that I was capable of keeping the store in order and that it would open, close and deliver some basic revenue stability.

In my experience, a lot of managers fail to acknowledge the power of good followership. Often, the highly assertive, powerful and vocal leader is the aspiration. In reality, the best thing to do is execute processes in line with company expectations and learn the ropes, with a dose of critical thinking and autonomy thrown in. With this, moments of flow and synchronisation are felt throughout a team. Those isolated moments of execution, quality communication and teamwork begin to happen.

The problem is that once the learning and reliability are established, a ceiling forms, prohibiting the motivational, inspirational and innovative abilities that would take the follower leader to the next level in the leadership journey. Followers rarely initiate or develop new and improved solutions, and are left wanting whenever a new challenge comes their way.

The danger of followership is that it can slip into a zone of comfort and aimlessness, paving the way back to existor leadership. When we follow for too long or lose our ability to think critically, our followership becomes purposeless, principle-less and agenda-less. It is a mentality I still regularly find myself slipping into. When we always look to others to tell us what to do, we give away our power. We feel we are not capable or strong enough to make decisions ourselves. Stepping into our responsibilities and taking a proactive approach to our work and team performance is a decisive step that will ensure we maintain our forward propulsion on our leadership journey.

The reliable style of a follower maintains steady results. But to graduate from follower leadership, we need to be more active, take more chances and experiment more. This is best done in small steps and with a high level of communication with superiors. With the durability of a survivor, the agreeableness of an existor and the capability and reliability of a follower, the leader has a strong base from which to graduate into the higher-functioning modes of leadership. This is where real rhythm and synchronisation can be seeded and grown.

Motivators – Engaged Leadership

In the past decade, there has been a lot of talk about engagement as the essential element of productivity. A swag of research from many corners has confirmed that when people are wholly focused on one task, all sorts of brain chemistry lights up and feel-good hormones are released into our system. The concept of *being in the zone* is one way of describing this. And when that level of engagement is achieved across teams of people, then quality, efficiency and productivity skyrocket.

Gallup research quantifies the effect of engaged employees: they produce 18% more productivity and contribute an increase of 12% in profitability.[35] Imagine if everyone was engaged in their work. No wonder human resource professionals have been focusing on engagement metrics and lifting engagement as a primary business pillar.

So, how can leaders engage people? What can a leader do to lift engagement in their team? And what does it look like?

Jim Collins refers to *level 5 leaders* in his book, *Good to Great*.[36] In business leadership, Collin's work has become a standard reference. Collins and his team collated the common threads shared between the leaders of corporate organisations that had sustained astronomical share-price growth. Collins found that the very best leaders *"were more like Lincoln and Socrates than Patton or Caesar."* This is another way of saying the top echelon of leaders showed care and attention towards their people, rather than dictating to them. The best leaders listen, empathise and create understanding between themselves and their people, and all stakeholders. It can sound airy fairy, but it is grounded in practical, tangible ways of working that create engaged teams. And engaged teams are full of motivated people.

Motivational leaders are often seen as big personalities with booming voices, high energy and huge presence. They shake the world with boundary-breaking thinking and amazing feats of heroism. But this stereotype is not the reality. It is also not useful for us mere mortals who do not have these natural gifts but aspire to be high-performing leaders.

During my five years of research on this subject before writing this book, I found that the above description is a myth. It applies to the heroes of blockbuster movies, whose primary purpose is to entertain, enthral and wow audiences. Let's face it, people sitting around, talking deeply and considerately to solve problems do not make for riveting entertainment. Blow-ups like Steve Jobs are much more entertaining than the quiet, shy and seemingly ordinary leaders, like Darwin E. Smith. Smith was the CEO of Kimberly-Clark (a paper-based consumer products company) for 20 years, leading the business to outperform the general stock market by four times. Smith's tenure generated growth that dwarfed Procter & Gamble, Coca-Cola and General Electric over the same period.

What is it that *motivator* leaders do? They engage their staff. They make every individual feel important, loved and that they belong. This connectedness feeds directly into individual motivation. Motivators engage people's hearts and minds. They show care for the team, which translates into the team caring more for their projects. It is like Alex Pentland's concept of vulnerability loops – when one person opens up and shows vulnerability, other people feel comfortable to do the same. The motivator leader creates a motivational loop.

Motivation is a complex art as much as it is a science. It is individual to all of us, but it becomes easier for us as leaders when we realise what the outcome of motivation is: engagement. Keeping this in mind helps us understand why we are creating space for listening, caring and understanding. It gives us a practical reason to stop or slow our pace and that of our team. This is at the heart of the facilitation meme, *"Go slow to go fast,"* and is fundamental to lowering team members' mental unease and doubts, which can derail any chance of flow and ongoing rhythm.[37]

Motivational leaders understand this and, therefore, can channel their energy towards this outcome. They know that their primary job is to hunt the people I call *get its* – staff who don't need to be educated on why they are doing what they are doing. They are the sort of people we don't need to constantly check in on to make sure they are doing what needs to be done. The get its get how they are going to do their work and instinctively know why it matters. They get what impact their work will have. Motivator leaders keep these people humming along and never take them for granted. A motivator also knows they need to hunt the *don't get its*, and snuff them out with deep conversation. No stone is left unturned in this pursuit of identification and conversion.

I have found that motivator leaders in our contemporary workplaces engage staff through the consistent practice of *coaching*. Modern coaching is a great first step to becoming a motivator leader. It is tremendously powerful when a leader sees themselves as a coach whose purpose is to help their staff get to where they want to be. From this position, a leader has a high impact on performance and on lives. It is truly inspirational. Elite sporting coaches and managers across male professional codes are often quoted as not just wanting to have a team full of champion players, but a culture of good humans; young men who are good sons, brothers, husbands and dads. The traditional view of keeping the professional and personal separate still exists, but with a caveat: we are dealing with humans, so we must speak to the whole human and not just the professional two-dimensional bit we see during the working week. Your team members are not robots – they are emotional beings making hundreds of split-second decisions with many emotions attached to them.

When we work with a leader who genuinely cares about us, we find ourselves caring more about our work. We're more committed and, therefore, more engaged. An embedded cycle of accountability comes with this. If my boss cares deeply about my work and is willing to listen to me, then I must be prepared to be questioned about what I say and do. Once again, this contributes to an environment of high performance. Motivators are wonderful leaders, and to generate high-performing teams, they engage people through daily human-to-human conversation. When a leader leverages this to motivate teams during difficult times, they bring home results with much less friction and a lot more rhythm.

A common problem with motivator leadership is that it takes a lot of investment. There is a toll. With so much individual attention required across the team, the leader must invest huge amounts of time. This means being willing to sacrifice their lifestyle, time with their family and time to work on their pet projects (or areas of work they are good at or enjoy).

As well as being time consuming, motivating teams is draining. It involves being present in every discussion, actively listening, crafting questions, and encouraging curiosity and debate. Motivators are continuously learning and holding the space for their team members' learning, which is mentally fatiguing. They are required to be decisive, but also to include other people and their ideas in their decision making. It is a balancing act that requires buckets of energy, patience and clear mindedness – all executed with a lot of planning, the delicate skill of diplomacy and steely toughness.

The only thing that will keep a motivator leader in the game is a true understanding of why their work matters. It is not for the faint hearted, and if the person is in the wrong job for the wrong reasons, they will not become the motivator leader they aspire to be. And even when motivator leaders are doing a great job, there is still a limit to how long they can keep it up. They may be able to bring in one project, deliver a phase of change or build a team, but being able to do these things multiple times may be beyond them due to the laborious style of this leadership. If rhythm was a circular flow, motivators could complete one cycle, but exhaustion may tear away at the edges of the team, making it difficult to maintain meaningful progress.

Motivating people to be highly engaged is a critical skill for all leaders to learn. To sustain results and build long-term performance, there are further leadership abilities to stack onto this growing foundation of excellence. If a leader is to create real rhythm that shuts the door on the old paradigm and ensures the new paradigm takes hold, they must gravitate towards a position where talent, customers, exciting challenges and new opportunities come to them, rather than having to hunt or compete for them. Motivators have earnt the right to play at the top table of rhythm. Here we go!

Attractors – Respected Leadership

What is the last thing you recommended to a friend? It could have been a place to go for dinner, a movie, an accountant who helped you with your last tax return, or a place to work. There is something powerful about giving a recommendation. It is meaningful and says a lot about us. In fact, it says everything about us. It shows people what we value and discloses a lot about our personality.

You could argue that there is nothing more personal than a recommendation. We have all been there when a friend recommends a physiotherapist, and he or she ends up being a bit rubbish. Or when a friend says the latest James Bond movie is brilliant, but you watch it and realise it is just another iteration of the '70s formula – outdated, irrelevant and full of unnecessary computer-animated explosions. In these moments, our opinion of our friend lowers ever so slightly. We think to ourselves, *"I won't be asking them for a recommendation again. They don't know what they're talking about when it comes to movies!"*

Recommendations are deeply personal. For this reason, the Net Promoter Score® (NPS) has become a standard metric for measuring customer service in the Western world. Since the NPS was devised by Fred Reichheld and his research team at Bain & Company in 2003, the question it asks customers has become a benchmarking tool for companies such as Australia Post, Apple Retail and American Express, amongst thousands of others. It asks one question:

> *"What is the likelihood that you would recommend Company X to a friend or colleague?"*

The customer answers with a rating out of 10. It is simple to implement and relates directly to how much a person truly values their customer experience. This tells us something profound about our willingness to recommend something to the people we like, love and spend time with. We need to be deeply confident in a product or company to tell our nearest and dearest to spend their time and money on it. And professionally, you could argue that the stakes are even higher. If you recommend a former colleague to get a job at a company you have just joined, it had better work out for them, or you put that person's career and everything that depends on it at risk.

What is it that makes us supremely confident that something is worth recommending? What must exist for this to occur? Not only intuitively, but practically?

The answer is respect; respect that has been built over many years. A proven track record that is credible and can be relied on. This is the power of *attractor* leadership. Attractors have proven that they can survive the tough times. They can fall into line as an existor when required. They can be excellent followers when they need to be helpful and productive. And they can be motivators and engage the people around them whenever they need to elevate care, move a team forward or bring people back on track.

Attractors have proven they can do these things dynamically and continually. They have built credibility over the course of many projects with many people. Their reputation is unshakable and valuable.

Businesses that have built themselves into a type of cult are examples of this. It could be a retail store that stocks products or brands people cannot buy wholesale or anywhere else. It could be a band or musician who sells out concerts within minutes. Or it could be a restaurant that's impossible to get a table at or even to get takeaway from.

Whenever I go travelling, I ask for recommendations from everyone I know. I canvas high and low for a selection of weird and wonderful things to see and do – things that are different from the typical stuff you'll find on Tripadvisor. It amazed me how many people said, *"You need to go to Fergburger,"* when I was going on a holiday to New Zealand. All of them said I should expect to line up for at least 45 minutes at this high-end burger joint in Queenstown, but it would be worth it. My initial response to this was, *"Whatever! I'm not interested in those sorts of gimmicks."* Usually, they end up being over-hyped and disappointing, full of annoying tourists and even more annoying staff. On our trip, a guide told me to go to another burger place down the road. *"It's better,"* they said. When I got to Queenstown, it was raining, so we were limited in what we could do. So, we thought we would check out one of the burger places. When it came to the crunch, I found myself intrigued and curious to see what all the Fergburger fuss was about. I ditched the idea of going to the other place and decided to stand in the rain, queuing with all the other suckers at Fergburger. I found myself not even knowing why I was queuing. It felt a little silly.

As we approached the entrance, the staff were going up and down the queue, handing out umbrellas and lollies. They seemed friendly, and the general vibe was pretty relaxed. Everyone was smiling; there was no angst. When we got inside, the small space was packed. I could see the ordering process and, somehow, it seemed to be working. We were served quite quickly and easily. We could even order a draught beer on tap while we waited. We patiently stood and watched the craziness unfold, and were lucky to get a seat right in front of the service area at the bar. The buzz and energy of the place was something else. We got our burgers and tucked in.

It was good. Really good. But the experience was better. Famous New York restaurateur Danny Meyer is known for asking his staff to *"create food raves"* in his restaurants, where everyone has a great time – like being at a dance party, but without the loud music and lighting show. I wasn't always sure what he was talking about until this experience. It was exactly what I felt Fergburger was doing. They were throwing a food rave! It was fun, interesting and exciting, and you felt like you were having a shared experience with everyone else. The staff were on fire and worked with big smiles in a beautiful sequence with each other. Their operation was a great example of a team with high synchronisation. The rhythm was fascinating to watch. They were doing a tremendous amount of work with ease and a smile on their faces. And the customer experience was unique and memorable. I loved it!

Fergburger is an attractor business that does not have to advertise or hunt for staff or customers. An attractor leader achieves the same thing in their teams. They build and maintain a working culture that is enjoyable to work in and is devastatingly productive and profitable. They attract talent and ensure the best staff members want to stay and do their best work. In turn, the attractor leader attracts external stakeholders, including clients and customers. An affinity is created with a gravitational pull of its own.

It is unrealistic to think this can be achieved in an instant. Some people can accelerate themselves to this type of leadership (which is what I want for you by sharing the key ingredients of the Rhythm Effect). No matter how long or short it takes, this is where a dramatic shift in a leader's profile and output happens. Their ability to deliver excellence and consistency elevates significantly, yet they work less and with less strain than all the previous leadership styles put together. Attractors create a culture where everyone is so committed and in tune with each other that a multitude of problems simply do not exist. These leaders must be 100% focused and on point, but the volume of work required to gain results is drastically reduced because their staff and clients are motivated the point of advocation. A clear and unapologetic identity has been formed.

An excellent example of an attractor is Jeff Bezos, CEO at Amazon. Whole populations want to work with him and his platform. The staff are called Amazonians, and their commitment to the cause is borderline cultish. Meanwhile, Google has Googlers. Disneyland has Cast Members. I am not saying these businesses are the most ethical or that we should all aim for their business models. But they are examples of high-impact entities in their fields, having built significant momentum over decades. They attract talent and customers at ever-increasing rates with growing commitment. The unstoppable momentum they have formed over generations has transformed into a contagious rhythm. They have built cultures of attraction, with attractor leaders who rely less on marketing spend and recruitments drives and more on a respected reputation with gravitational pull.

Attractors are ultra clear on who they are and who they serve. They establish long-term, frictionless ways of working. They have an unwavering intent to achieve their goals, and everyone in their team is highly skilled and committed to bringing these goals to fruition. Attractor leaders have consolidated the key ingredients of their business and developed a team of conscientious, service-minded team members. But to leave it at that would undermine the attractor. They also ask the big questions. They are unrelentingly curious. Their combined assertiveness and generosity means they are always observing, developing and understanding all stakeholders. And most importantly, the attractor synchronises them, like a conductor of an orchestra.

Powerful yet in service. Assertive yet accountable. Totally respected yet totally respectful. The pathway to progressor leadership is almost complete. Ongoing rhythm is now in play, with only one opportunity left to leverage: acceleration.

Progressors – Trusted Leadership

Anand Giridharadas is an American writer who, in his book, *Winners Take All: The Elite Charade of Changing the World*, describes a successful society as a *"progress machine"*. I like this definition, and my experience has told me that this is the noblest, most meaningful pinnacle any entity can aspire to. I feel that the businesses we run can all be progress machines. In turn, the leaders who drive them must be *progressor* leaders.

In the leadership models I have studied, I have found that most peak at the motivator or equivalent thereof. It's generally considered that the leader's job is to motivate, and if they can do this, then they are at the top of their game. I agree that the ability to motivate is integral to leadership, but we also need to consider the ability to create impact without a human, social or corporate toll. To avoid these tolls and achieve systematic excellence with a high ROE, a leader must hold a key set of skills and practices beyond motivation. This skillset goes beyond diligent strategy and is often difficult to describe. Some may say it is *"to have the magic touch"*; the intangible ju-ju we think some people have and some do not. Maybe we are just talking about people who have a bit of luck!

My work leads me to believe that progressor leaders have the full package. They bring their people along on the journey and build incredible momentum, like a snowball rolling down a mountain in a cartoon. It keeps going, getting bigger and bigger. It's unstoppable; an endless amount of energy that keeps gathering and moving forward. Occasionally, the progressor and their team may crash into a setback or some poor results. Still, the main thing is that equity, inclusion and benefits for all stakeholders are experienced and developed. Everyone achieves growth, and progress becomes systemic.

The closest term I can find to describe this culture is the Japanese concept of *"ikigai"*. From the Heian period (794 to 1185), it comprises two words: "iki" meaning "life", and "kai" meaning "effect", "result", "worth" or "benefit". I think a state of ikigai is important for us as leaders to aspire to, as the all-too-real pressures of daily capitalist life constantly distract our attention towards short-term goals and KPIs. We continually compromise to get results over the line, and I feel at times, it is forgivable (if not entirely expected) to sacrifice ideals to simply get the job done so we can all live another day.

But that is survivor leadership. We can do better than operating in this mode until something pops. *You* can do better. No matter how dire our situation is, if we do the work in the right areas, we can climb out of the mud of survival and slowly trek our way towards progressor leadership. We can attain this promised land of ikigai, often referred to as *"a reason to get out of bed,"* which is more valuable than it may seem.

As leaders, we have all experienced not wanting to get out of bed to go to work (Monday dread). We all have had a staff member call in sick when, really, they just don't want to come into work, or worse, they are going for a job interview at another company! I know I have done this a few times in my career. It is a classic sign that ikigai is missing. Even when results are strong, something is not right about what we are doing or, more importantly, how we are doing it.

I propose that we all have the ability to stop, take stock and put into place the necessary steps to form meaningful progress. We all have the opportunity to become progressor leaders within our own context. We do not all have to put a *"ding in the universe,"* as was the mission of Steve Jobs; we may become a progressor leader for our local tennis club. That would be amazing for the local community and would touch many people's lives. I believe we are all able to drive ROE up to the point of achieving daily synchronisation between junior and senior staff, between departments, and between external stakeholders, from shareholders to end users of our products.

A contemporary example of this is my dearly beloved Liverpool Football Club (LFC). Anyone who knows me knows I am extremely passionate about soccer, and LFC has been my team since I was a little kid. I don't know why a youngster growing up in the Adelaide Hills in South Australia would become so connected and attached to a team on the other side of the world. But it started with my mother ordering *Shoot Magazine* directly from the UK for my brother and me. I ended up with a stack of these magazines under my bed. At the time, there was one Australian playing in the English Football League: Craig Johntson. This was enough of a connection to make LFC my team, especially as it was winning at the time and garnered a lot of headlines. It was a relationship that would develop and become a meaningful part of my life; at least, in the context of leisure and entertainment. But being an LFC supporter has been a mostly sour experience in my adult life.

Since the dominant decades of the '70s and '80s, LFC went from a European powerhouse to a perennial second-rate contender. The type of contender that never quite made it back to its former glory. A club that continually decreased in power, presence and popularity. Even though it remained a big name in world sport, its reputation tarnished over three decades, during which time it did not win the league title once. It won a few major trophies other than the league, which was great, but the league is the one every club wants to win. It is the focal point of every season, and with poor results time and time again, LFC slipped out of qualification for other tournaments, losing corporate sponsorship and being unable to compete for the most talented players on the circuit.

Does this sort of scenario sound familiar? Do you ever feel that you cannot compete with the bigger competitors for market share, talent or recognition? This was the situation Jürgen Klopp came into when he took charge of the LFC football department in 2015. The club had come within a whisker of going into administration due to terrible mismanagement by the previous owners. The new owners, Fenway Sports Group (FSG), were slowly getting the house back in order when Klopp was appointed. The turnaround since then has been phenomenal.

In Klopp's first press conference, he stated that Liverpool would win the league title within four seasons.[38] It was the type of statement that simultaneously filled supporters like myself with optimism and terror, as we had seen so many false dawns throughout the years. In the coming years, the team slowly progressed up the ladder. It cemented its place in the premium yearly European cup competition (the Champions League) and went on to appear in two consecutive finals, winning in the latter in 2019. LFC also financially stabilised, then thrived.[39] As a close observer, it has been wonderful to see this organisation put into place a lot of the concepts I have researched for *The Rhythm Effect*.

Not only has LFC become a successful football team on the field, but it has also managed to do it by spending less than its wealthier competitors. In fact, the club's net spend on its playing squad in the five years between 2014–2018 was only the seventh highest in the league – half the spend of lowly contenders Brighton & Hove Albion, and more than five times less than its main rival, Manchester City, over the same period.[40]

Of course, Klopp has not done this alone. The club's sporting director, Michael Edwards, has been a genius in the area of recruitment and has struck brilliant transfer deals (a signal of synchronisation). LFC has been able to increase engagement with fan groups (local and global) and repair relationships, which helped it to make better decisions. The club has become a corporate sponsorship leader by attracting some of the biggest and best deals in world football, including a reported manufacturing deal for the LFC uniform with Nike, which will become the richest deal of its kind in English football history.[41] And the performance of the team itself is devastating (in a good way). The players are scintillating to watch, and it was by far the most exciting club team in England over the course of the 2018/19 season.[*]

When COVID-19 interrupted our lives in the closing months of the 2019/20 season, LFC was 25 points ahead of second place. To put that into perspective, at time of writing, Liverpool has 10 games of the season to play (if world events allow), and the previous record for the winning margin for the title was 19 points.[**] To say that LFC has been brilliant is an understatement. It is an amazing way to break a 29-year drought, but the real story here is the outstanding leadership of the organisation's highest-profile leader: Klopp. He has been able to bring every single stakeholder on board. He has not always been the nicest guy or got all the decisions right. But he has been able to communicate, listen and engage with everyone the whole time he has been there. He has aligned the football department with the commercial department, and he has been transparent and authentic in his communication with the football community and fan base.[42] It is a true example of what happens when all departments and stakeholder groups synchronise.

Klopp has become the pin-up boy for progressor leadership. He has achieved all his KPIs using fewer resources than his competitors, as well as those who previously filled his role at the club. He transformed the culture of the football department and updated the identity of the club in general, while honouring its past. He led the emergence of a new mindset that is rooted in togetherness and toughness yet energised by a freeness for all to express themselves. Player decision making, autonomy and discipline are ingrained in the team. Winning traditions have weighed heavily on many generations of squads since the "good old days", but Klopp has been able to help everyone detach from these unhelpful expectations, replacing them with a relevant purpose that everyone is completely committed to. Internally, he aligns daily sessions with a broad mission wrapped in the highest of ambitions. Klopp continually speaks of the team *being in rhythm* as a key indicator

[*] After the 2019/20 season resumed during the COVID-19 crisis, LFC went on to win the Premier League Championship under Jürgen Klopp – the first time the club had won this title since 1990.

[**] Liverpool was able to go on and win the English Premier League once officials deemed it safe to continue playing in the face of the COVID-19 pandemic.

of the team playing well.[43] How did Klopp do this? He is deeply trusted. I have been observing Klopp in hundreds of interviews over the years. Without exception, he is transparent, honest and consistent. He does not say things to toe the company line. He does not spout the usual clichés you hear in modern professional sport. He does not pretend to have all the answers, and he knows it is not his job to have them. He is known to drop the occasional S or F bomb in interviews, showing a human side to his personality. Klopp speaks his mind yet does not take responsibility for others' decisions or work. He does not speak to further his own cause. A good example of this is the way he speaks out about fixture congestion.

Modern European football leagues are big-money industries, and football administrators know this. The more matches the big stars play, the more money they get through sponsorship and extraordinary television deals. So, the top players now live a life where it is rare for them to get any form of rest. During the season, they play multiple times a week, meaning that teams do not even get to train as much as they need to, let alone recover properly. During the supposed offseason, a lot of international tournaments are played. It is a great way to exhaust the very people on whom all revenue relies. This sets up the potential for standards of play to drop, more injuries and shorter careers. The so-called leaders are slowly choking their golden goose.

At a time when Klopp is winning and has more resources than most to cope with such an environment, he remains staunch and abrasive in his opinion on the subject. It is a sign of integrity. It shows that self-interest is not his source of motivation. He wants his players to have the healthiest lives possible. He wants football, the sport he loves, to be healthy. And he wants the entire football community to flourish for many generations to come. His constant campaigning contributed to officials inserting a small *winter break* in the English Premier League's season for the first time.[44] It is a small shift, but it is industry progress. The most important thing is that Klopp has gained the wholehearted trust of his players, his staff, his board and the wider football community. It is the type of leadership we can all aspire to. It is simple in theory, yet the journey is lined with treacherous landmines. Delicate balance is, once again, a factor of this level of leadership, and knowing the select skills needed to achieve this balance is critical. Otherwise, trust swiftly diminishes.

Almost every single person involved with the LFC has benefited from Klopp's style of trust, where he has upheld a culture of family instead of a group of work colleagues. However, Klopp and FSG (the owners of the club) still have work to do. An example of this is the need to invest in and support the LFC female team. It is well below that of many competitors in the league, and if anything is a blight on the current record of the LFC leaders, it is this. It shows us that even progressor leaders have room for improvement. But that is the point. It is not about perfection or ticking every box. The point of achieving the Rhythm Effect is that it is never ending. There is always more to do, and a progressor leader understands this.

The next challenges are exciting and energising for everyone involved. There is no need for judgement; there is only a need for action, creativity and exploration. We need a mindset that focuses on maintaining systemic synchronisation, not only for the team we work with, but for generations to come. Progressors teach people how to achieve this mindset. They show others the benefits of rhythm and synchronisation and how to achieve it. The possibilities are infinite when leaders motivate, attract and progress their communities. And the opportunity is there for all of us.

This leadership journey from transactional to trusted is accessible to us all, but it takes a specific set of proficiencies and competencies that a leader must learn, practise and master. Only then will they be able to run their own workflow with minimal friction and get into cycles of rhythm. Only then will they be able to synchronise the people in their teams to create accelerated progress. It is a large body of work, but if you are up for the challenge, there are significant personal, professional and cultural rewards to enjoy.

The next step is to learn about the building blocks of rhythm.

The Building Blocks of Rhythm

"It is only by practise that you can understand the events of life and find the right rhythm. Once you get into the rhythm of life, you can flow with life and enjoy happiness effortlessly."
– Awdhesh Singh

The Ingredients

The first thing that comes to people's minds when you mention rhythm is music. We often talk of people having "great rhythm" or comment on a song having "a nice rhythm to it". In professional sport, I often hear players and coaches talk of being "in" or "out" of rhythm as a reason for their success or failure in a match.

But what are people actually talking about? Rhythm is one of those things everyone understands yet finds difficult to define. And when asked what the ingredients of rhythm are, most would struggle to give a concise answer.

A music teacher I spoke to on the subject gave me an insightful response:

1. **Rhythm is a succession of strong and weak elements.** What a wonderfully simple yet in-depth starting point. The word "succession" speaks of an ongoing and repeatable nature. The mention of strong and weak elements refers to the ups and

downs, loud and quiet, hard and soft, sharp and dull. This tells us that rhythm is not one-paced. It requires opposites and counterbalances. Rhythm cannot be high, fast or strong all the time – a good thing to remember when thinking about workplace performance.

2. **Rhythm requires timing with accuracy on a regular beat.** There is no point hitting the right note if the note is played at the wrong time. Timing is essential and must be overlayed with accuracy; not just once, but regularly. Having a sense of what needs to be done at a specific time is crucial to harvesting rhythm. It is a precision pattern of movement. In any context, rhythm requires the management of one's environment, self and relationships.

3. **Rhythm is synchronisation with an ensemble.** It is not only the drummer who requires rhythm but everyone in a band. Everyone needs to play to the same tune. Everyone must rely on each other to hit the right note at the same tempo. If there is no synchronisation, it is a mess. There is no time to discuss whether a beat will be hit – it just needs to happen. The moment a guitarist strums their strings, the ivory keys need to be hit by the piano player. A micro-second early or late upsets the whole performance. Playing to your own tune, tempo and pitch throws others out of rhythm and, in turn, will throw you out of rhythm. To be in rhythm, we must be in synchronisation with our tools and teammates. This is non-negotiable.

What are the reasons why musicians can fail to create and sustain rhythm?[45]

1. **Level of skill.** When the skill level of a musician is not high enough to play a particular track, rhythm is impossible. This is why I gave up guitar lessons within a year of starting when I was in primary school. My fingers wouldn't move as quickly as I wanted them to. Instead of concentrating on the music, I was continually looking at my fingers, getting behind, trying to figure out the next chord I had to somehow get my fingers to create. At this point, there was

no chance of getting into rhythm as a guitarist. Just like any of us learning a new skill, such as driving or a new process at work, we need the technical skills or we are at sea.

2. **Complexity of the composition.** Like anything in life, the world of music contains simple scenarios and more complex ones. Playing "Row, Row, Row Your Boat" on the guitar was within my scope as a schoolboy guitarist. My guitar teacher, Mrs Smith, would have been happy for us to belt out a chorus of this old ditty any day of the week. But give us anything a little harder, and we would have sunk. This happens to all of us. Filling out a tax return for an individual wage earner with no tax deductions is easy for an entry-level accountant. But give them the responsibility of managing the tax returns of a local construction company with 20 employees, and there will be panic. Rhythm can only be achieved when the level of complex layers within any song (or job) can be seen, understood and executed. In our workplaces, this requires not only technical skills but also analytical skills, as the complexity comes in the form of decision making and thinking through problems without hesitation or doubt.

3. **The experience is exasperating.** Enjoyment is low. Maybe the reason for playing is unclear, or what you are playing is not fun. This may be because it is too hard or boring. Maybe the young piano player prefers jazz instead of classical. Maybe the lead guitarist has outgrown his bandmates and is ready for a bigger stage. Exasperation can come in many forms, and it is difficult to synchronise and uphold rhythm when you'd rather be somewhere else. No matter whether the job is too easy or hard, you don't get along with the other band members, or, more importantly, you do not believe in the work anymore, if the experience is stressful or a drag, then it will be near impossible to be in rhythm. Mature social skills will help us understand and manage this, especially as leaders in a team environment.

To overcome these obstacles to rhythm, there are three *building blocks* we need to focus on as leaders of a team, both for ourselves and the people in our teams.

The Three Building Blocks of Rhythm

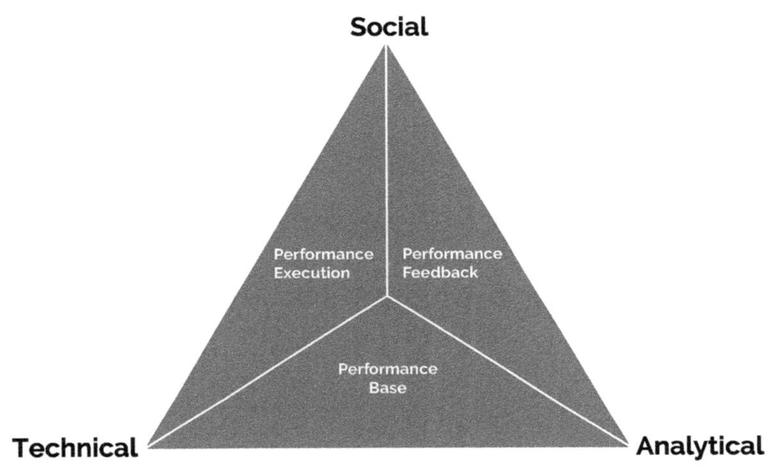

The first building block is the *technical proficiencies* of a job. If we cannot perform a role, then we will fumble through our work. The ability to hit the right notes with precision will be impossible. Think of technical proficiencies as the "hands" of rhythm.

Then there are the *analytical proficiencies* of our work. We need to understand and align the many factors of our business. What are we doing? Why are we doing what we are doing and how are we doing it? When should initiatives be done? Being able to wrap the most relevant metrics around these factors is essential; otherwise, the complexity will be difficult to communicate and discuss. There'll be no chance of everyone in a team or organisation being in harmony with each other if they are unable to think through and make sense of the complex elements of the business. Think of analytical proficiencies as the "brain" of rhythm.

Finally, there are the *social proficiencies*. This is the ability to feel and sense others and to manage emotions and reactions to environmental factors. At the end of the day, you feel rhythm. It's the ability to trust that others will strike that note at the precise moment you need them to. Rhythm requires a sense of place in the context of others and the intended audience. It also requires a streak of daring, and it demands complete attention. Think of social proficiencies as the "heart" of rhythm.

Let's take a look at these three building blocks of rhythm in detail.

Technical Proficiencies

Modern professional roles are complex. For this reason, our self-management and relationship management skills are becoming more and more important. But before we delve into such waters, we need to have a good, old-fashioned audit of our skills. The hard skills required in a job may be an obvious place to start, but they are often overlooked, maybe because they are too obvious. Many of us have had the experience of taking a training course and, two weeks later, reverting to our old ways of doing things. Old habits die hard.

Abraham Lincoln is attributed with saying, *"Give me six hours to chop down a tree and I will spend the first four sharpening the axe."* This quote is often used to emphasise the importance of strategy in business, but I think of the axe as being our hard skills. If they are not sharp, we will have to work very hard for a poor result. So, the first step is to get brutally honest regarding our hard skills

When I was a cricketer, I did not have the defensive technique to become a good batsman. When I was a salesperson, my sales pitch did not have a good enough process to sell more promotions into my accounts. When I was a corporate sales manager, my Microsoft Excel skill level was not good enough to keep me on top of the complex metrics of the business. If I had mastered these hard skills, my performance would have improved significantly. My ROE would have skyrocketed.

It seems to me that many people are not honest enough to confess to their (and their team's) limitations and lack of skills. This can be driven by pride or apathy. Furthermore, time and resources need to be poured into upskilling, and there is the risk this will result in little change or even lowered performance, as per the consolidation phase (see Chapter 3). Whatever the case, I have still always found that doing a skills audit is a good idea. Awareness on this front is helpful. Talking openly about it is even better. Ultimately, taking action to improve and master skills will bring us closer to building rhythm within our teams; otherwise, we doubt ourselves or wait to be caught out. Deep down, if we know we are not able to execute a particular skill within our work, we are left hoping our limitation will not be exposed. This fear is enough to distract our focus and inhibit flow. Inadvertently, we make work harder for ourselves and live in a low ROE state.

As leaders, there are industry-specific skills we need to be proficient in. I call these the *unique technical skills* for your industry, location or specific role. We may not need to be able to do the jobs of our team, but we need to have knowledge of them and understand the details. This not only makes us more confident leaders, but it also gives us credibility with our people. In a 2011 study of CEOs of hospitals in the US,[46] researchers posed the question:

> *Are hospitals ranked more highly when they are led by medically trained doctors or non-MD professional managers?*

The resulting hospital quality scores (the key metric to answering this question) of the hospitals with doctors as CEOs were 25% higher than those of the other hospitals. One reason is that these CEOs had more credibility with staff. They were domain experts and, therefore, *expert leaders*. The idea of expert leaders being higher-performing leaders is constant across many studies of organisational performance. No matter the industry or territory, if you have the technical skills of the domain you are leading, you will be in a better position to lead high-performing cultures.

Working more than a decade in the salon industry showed me this. Non-hairdresser salon owners tended to be the ones who struggled to build and maintain their businesses. It was too easy for the staff to pull the wool over their eyes. When they made decisions, the technically talented staff members were often judgmental and derisive, or the senior hairstylists would be overly relied upon for their opinion in key decisions. It was not a foundation for success.

Being technically proficient in your role and understanding your team's technical roles are critical to synchronisation and building a rhythmic team.

Then there are the *universal technical skills* for leaders. These are the skills a leader needs to manage the various day-to-day interactions and scenarios they face. They are often categorised as people management or relationship management proficiencies, but I believe they fall under the category of universal technical skills. The reason for this is that anyone in a leadership position can develop them – they are processes that can be learnt in the same way we learn mathematics or how to use a new software platform. I have boiled them down to the following list. I know there are more, but if a leader has strong proficiency in these skills, they will be able to tackle most challenges confidently:

1. **Timeline management.** Everyone is time poor. The leader's ability to prioritise and organise workflows for themselves and others is central to finding rhythm. Pillar systems, robust boundaries and clear communication halt the slide into survivor leadership.

2. **Performance management.** Tracking and mentoring staff to support and encourage performance, as well as having a strong process for transitioning staff out of a team when required. This is often delicate and sometimes requires engagement with human resources or exterior stakeholders. A strong knowledge of company policies, legislation and management best practice can save a team culture and individual relationships from becoming toxic and annihilating any chance of synchronisation.

3. **Succession planning.** Setting up and executing a long-term framework to build emerging leaders and high-performing technical staff. This nurtures a robust and efficient business of today, as well as a strong and powerful business of tomorrow. Succession planning bolsters short-term performance and safeguards long-term profitability, making the team more capable should disaster strike. Ask yourself: *If I broke my leg, how would the team do without me for eight weeks?* If the answer sends a shudder down your spine, then it needs addressing.

4. **Delegation.** When a leader increases the responsibilities of their people to create succession and lower their over-reliance on the leader. Too often, however, delegation is another word for palming off work we are too busy to do or don't want to do. This creates tension, strain and mistakes, leading to loss of clients, staff and/ or respect, plummeting the leader back into the extinction phase (see Chapter 3).

5. **Effective conversations.** A leader must understand the structure and characteristics of a good-quality conversation. Without the ability to hold effective discussions, it is difficult for a leader to gain respect and encourage a safe and trusting environment. Without good-quality conversational skills, the entire team's communication can be jagged, inconsistent and unbalanced, making rhythm impossible to obtain individually and collectively.

6. **Negotiation.** The ability to engage with all kinds of stakeholders to find win-win agreements in the small daily scenarios, as well as for business-changing deals and initiatives. Being able to prepare, manage and hold oneself in a negotiation for positive outcomes is a skill that comes with experience, but having training or mentoring in this area with a clear process is helpful. One bad negotiation can cause good people to struggle in extinction for years, harming reputations and business performance long after a leader has left a team.

7. **Effective one-on-ones.** These include informal and formal one-on-one reviews. Holding these regularly and making sure they are practical and meaningful will engage staff and keep them focused, as opposed to simply working through a tick-box exercise. When done well, everyone's purpose and enjoyment of their work grows, and hundreds of hours are saved across a team over the course of a year – possibly thousands for larger teams!

8. **Coaching.** Have coaching conversations with others so they can find their own solutions and take majority ownership over their goals and achievements. We know coaching is fundamental to motivator leadership (Chapter 4), and being able to execute this with various stakeholders in all sorts of scenarios elevates one's leadership to a place where engagement and respect compound.

9. **Feedback.** Having a reliable feedback mechanism to use with staff daily ensures clean and clear communication to validate performance. It creates a learning environment with little space for ambiguity to breed. Good feedback loops grease the wheels of a team and are imperative for a leader. Without feedback, it is impossible to make clear and accurate decisions, and everyone's growth is severely dulled.

10. **Mastering meetings.** Ensuring meetings keep to time and are focused and inclusive. Having a robust process for before, during and after meetings will ensure they are tools for productivity and cohesion, instead of tools for degradation and wasted time. Meetings can become time pits in everyone's schedules and are a huge drain on a leader's mental resources. When a leader excels in this skill, their team's engagement and productivity shift dramatically forward.

11. **Assertiveness.** Often misunderstood and seen as an emotional intelligence skill, assertiveness is a key technical framework for all leaders to understand and master. Being able to maintain equality, consistency and quality in a team's interactions is fundamental to the success of any leader. When charged with dealing with difficult

or awkward personalities, assertiveness is what helps leaders to create trust. Assertiveness is particularly important in managing upward relationships and ensuring interactions with senior staff are strong and respectful rather than scary and limiting.

12. **Confrontation.** The ability to spot, initiate and utilise confrontation to create new learnings, cohesion and innovation. Done well, confrontation can open dialogue and calm people rather than be a combative experience, which most people associate with confrontation in the workplace.

13. **Problem-solving facilitation.** A robust process for holding conversations and leading the team through a challenge to find solutions. The leader uses a problem-solving canvas to extract the team's expertise on a subject to collate, synthesise and agree on solutions. It is critical to avoid knee-jerk and simplistic solutions to the complex problems we face in our workplaces. Without problem-solving facilitation, survival leadership (see Chapter 4) will be a common experience.

After years of learning the above universal technical skills in various leadership roles, I have gone on to deliver courses on each of them and still do to this day. They are fundamentals all leaders need to know, understand and practise to increase their ROE and that of their team. I am aware this is not an exhaustive list of skills and am sure others could be added, but it is a strong list of leadership skills nonetheless.

If there is anything on this list you do not feel confident with or have not been taught, then stop reading and organise some training or mentoring in these areas immediately. Your leadership will spring to life off the back of learning, practising and mastering these skills. They are a part of the *performance base* of rhythm. You will be equipped with the tools you need to face any scenario thrown at you. The social proficiencies help us execute them at a whole new level, but before we concern ourselves with this, firstly, we must learn the above suite of skills and build them into our daily way of leading. If not, it will be almost impossible to move beyond survivor leadership and the extinction phase of ROE.

Analytical Proficiencies

"Why the hell am I doing this?" This is a question I often ask myself when I play golf. It is a time-consuming activity full of frustration and can leave me feeling mentally exhausted and physically shot. It can be an expensive pastime, too. As a social golfer, there is no chance of me entering a local competition, let alone becoming a professional. Then there is the opportunity cost. I could use the time to read, go to the beach with friends, be with my family or go on holiday instead of playing this weird and masochistic game. So, why do I do it?

It is a feeling many of us have at our workplaces. Our rollercoaster of busy-ness, day after long day, can leave us wondering, *"What are we doing in the first place? Why are we slogging away? Why should we care? And why should others care?"* These are big questions many find difficult to answer. This is why companies have mission statements, vision statements and core values. When used properly, they are powerful and bring people together to perform well over generations. But often, a company's mission is contrived of meaningless buzzwords slapped together by people who either no longer work there or no one speaks to. They can be irrelevant to most workers and difficult to utilise for most leaders.

At the other end of the scale are the daily habits and behaviours everyone in a business needs to exhibit for the collective to be successful. For my golf game, it may include using the same pre-shot routine for every shot, switching off my mind from golf between shots, and keeping a smile on my face so I don't slide into a spiral of angst and frustration when I lose another ball! In a retail environment, team members may collectively agree that they will focus on performing three non-negotiable behaviours every day, which will help the team achieve its goals. This may include mentioning one relevant add-on product with every sale, focusing on cleanliness and perfect visual merchandising at all times, and actively calling loyal clients to let them know when the latest stock has arrived. These are simple-to-understand behaviours everyone can commit to. It's also easy for a leader to see whether they are happening every day.

Yet, most teams do not set out, agree upon, update or track these kinds of behaviours. I have found this to be common in most workplaces for one good reason: they are difficult to keep data on. This is especially true in a professional environment where you do not see other people working all the time. These behaviours are also highly intangible and near impossible to measure. Ever since Peter Drucker told us, *"If you can't measure it, you can't improve it,"* we have thrown out the idea of a leader purposefully getting their team to agree on, commit to and perform daily behaviours. It is too hard, so we have become obsessed with tangible things that can be measured. But there are problems with this.

Over more than two decades, I have observed that many businesses do not have alignment between their *mission* (the big picture telling everyone why the business exists) and the *moments* (the daily behaviours). They are both abstract and difficult to relate to tangible metrics. We are all too busy to talk about such nonsense, meaning that we see these things as "nice to haves" rather than "essential requirements". But I would argue that creating alignment between mission and moments is one of the biggest opportunities we have in our modern professional settings. Deep down, I think we all intellectually know this but are not sure how to go about investigating it, or we are simply preoccupied with a constant stream of urgencies.

In times of crisis, we put this conversation of alignment on the back burner and pour all our energies into the pressing issues of the day. Yet, this may be the one thing that seals the fate of professionals operating in the extinction phase. Being able to analytically observe these factors, patch them together, discuss them, and then find alignment puts a leader in an incredibly strong and powerful position. These are the *analytical proficiencies*. When partnered with the technical proficiencies, they create the performance base for our teams and organisations. Rhythm is possible with these fundamentals in place. When the performance base is strong in a leader, there is no hesitation, and all communication is clean, clear and consistent – a devastatingly powerful mix. As an extension to this, when the whole team has a strong performance base, real momentum is generated, and pure rhythm is possible.

Leaders need a deep understanding of the business so they can answer questions beyond a superficial level. Answering follow-up questions and the hard questions instils belief in everyone concerned. It is like a parent having a conversation with a persistent five-year-old who wants to paint pictures on the lounge room walls. It can be difficult to answer simple questions with completeness:

"Why can't I paint my picture on the walls?"

"Because it will make a mess!"

"So what?"

"Well, I don't want to have to clean it up."

"Whyyyyy?"

"Because I am busy doing other things for work."

"Whyyyyy?"

"Because I need to do work to pay for our home, clothes, food and school."

"Whyyyyy?"

"Aghhhhh!"

We can feel like this at work, too. When asked "why" after we've given instructions to our team or "why" they need to collate that extra report for the monthly meeting, it can be difficult to provide a clear, holistic answer. As opposed to the five-year-old, what makes matters worse is that professionals often do not ask all their questions because they don't want to look silly (or they restrain themselves out of perceived politeness). This can create tension, resentment and overall friction in the team. Often, a leader does not have the full story or a thorough understanding of every detail. So, when questioned, an element of "ducking and diving" needs to be done. This undermines trust and authority if done regularly or in high-stakes scenarios. The ability to connect everyday tasks with the big picture is extremely useful, and the difference between leaders who can garner deep trust and those who cannot.

As a facilitator, I have witnessed highly intelligent and hard-working professional leadership groups come to the conclusion that the problems they face are due to the following:

- *"We do it this way because we always have."*
- *"We do this stuff because the big boss tells us to."*
- *"It's too hard and expensive to change our process."*

Or my favourite:

- *"We're too busy!!!"*

In one case, we figured out that a company was wasting so much time duplicating information between different departments as part of their process, it added up to 1½ times a full-time wage over a year for this team! The waste was incredible! The above answers may seem cliched, but I am astounded as to how common they are. When pushed, many teams will find these are the real reasons why they do the things they do. Add layers of political manoeuvring and professional posturing, and the missed opportunities are extremely costly (i.e. extinction is inevitable).

A mechanism I use to iron out these misalignments is the *5xM Framework*. This links the mission to the moments in five steps. It is a great structure to use as a discussion point with a team and to plan action. Importantly, it paves the way for an ever-evolving conversation that gives a leader every opportunity to define and refine their team's performance strategy.

5XM Framework

		Lens	Focus	Criteria
1		Mission	What am I trying to achieve?	Independent
2		Milestone	What are my current period goals?	Relative
3		Measure	How do I know if I have achieved it?	Numeric
4		Mover	What are the key drivers of influence?	Initiatives
5		Moments	What are the daily traits that drive the drivers?	Observable

The 5xM Framework can be applied to individuals, teams, departments and organisations.* Let's look at it from a company perspective. The steps starting from the top are:

1. Mission: *"What are we trying to achieve?"*

This is independent of all other factors. It has nothing to do with "anniversarising" last year's figures or achieving a ranking in your industry. Your mission is the deep reason for doing what you do as a business. It's tougher to nail than it appears, but even simply regularly posing this question creates a richness of engagement and thought in all workers. Some may call this their credo or creed; others call it their higher purpose. It is a critical element of motivation and, when used well, it has a gravitational pull for staff, customers and communities.

2. Milestones: *"What are our current goals?"*

These are relative to previous results of the business, competitor activity and the environmental conditions of your industry. Milestones usually come in the form of a three-year strategy. It may be a mix of marketing, production and investment initiatives of sizable proportion that will

---

* I recommend every person uses this framework in relation to their career and update it at least every year. The clarity, confidence and motivation one can experience from this alone can be very impactful. Give it a go!

shape the business over the coming years. All publicly listed companies will have milestones in place, and national business affiliates will have them for their territory. SMEs may or may not have them in place. If they are in place, are they aligned with the mission and are they robustly referred to and updated? This is a big opportunity for many business leaders, as milestones provide a platform for everyone to be updated, clear and aligned with each other as things change and new challenges arise.

3. Measures: *"How do we know if we have achieved it?"*

These are numeric and refer to the tangible metrics most businesses obsess over. They are the budget forecasts and targets that have been put in place to measure performance. Run rates, key performance indicators, key risk indicators and net promoter scores are just a few examples of the endless acronyms and possible metric points our businesses can use. To Mr Drucker's point, measures are the tangible elements that give us a black-and-white answer to questions about our achievements. They matter and give us an independent reference point. And in a highly automated world, data is proving to be the biggest asset a business can have. I believe that measures are important, but we can overly focus on them compared to the other steps in the 5xM Framework. They are a means but not an end. Without context, they can even be meaningless. Altogether, the 5xMs ensure the measures have the context a leader needs so they can make clear and thoughtful decisions.

4. Movers: *"What are the key drivers of influence?"*

These are the initiatives we implement: short-term campaigns, battles and projects. For an apparel brand, a mover could be a promotional calendar that revolves around its spring/summer and autumn/winter collections. For a professional sporting team, a mover could be the selection policy for the upcoming year or the formation it will implement for the season. Whatever the guise, movers are tactically planned drivers of the business. These initiatives will be the focus of the measures and will, therefore, the be the main tools used across a business to drive towards milestones.

5. Moments: *"What are the daily traits that drive the drivers?"*

These are the observable things we see people do every day. *"After all is said and done, more is said than done"* – a famous quote attributed to Aesop from ancient Greece. All the 5xMs we've explored so far are nothing without the daily actions of everyone involved in a business to bring it alive. Action is the one constant none of us can escape. Yet we find it difficult to track and improve the consistent behaviours of our teams. Interpretations can be blurred, assumptions made and excuses heard. In the face of this, leaders tend to go with their gut and spend decades using trial and error to build ways of coping and eventually align the behaviours of staff.

On the other hand, the ability to isolate, articulate and embed a set of prioritised actions as a clear expectation of a team makes these behaviours non-negotiable. They're things everyone can execute and a leader can support with complete consistency. When aligned with all the other analytical work, moments become the fuel that organisational rhythm feeds on.

When the analytical proficiencies are understood and invested in, and alignment between the 5xMs is achieved, a team's performance skyrockets. There is no confusion about standards, expectations or where attention needs to be. The daily expression of the entire business can be truly aligned without any drag. People can crack on and work completely uninhibited. And if we think we do not have time to delve into these questions and crystallise our answers, then I call bullshit on that.

The aim of the game is to observe our businesses through the lens of these questions. This is an ongoing conversation you have with yourself and all stakeholders. It is not reserved for once a year when executives work through the battle plan for the following 12 months. It can be, but there is no value in that. The analytical proficiencies create a constant feedback loop that develops and becomes clearer over time.

Social Proficiencies

The technical proficiencies and analytical proficiencies create our *performance base*. When these building blocks are in place, we give ourselves every chance to do high-value work efficiently and enjoyably. We have full confidence in our skill level and the knowledge and assurance that we are equipped for the challenges ahead. As a team, this becomes almost exponential and is why the Rhythm Effect is such a powerful framework. We have the motivation that comes with knowing why we are doing what we are doing, and clarity on how this fits into our daily work.

But for these proficiencies to truly come alive, one more element is required. Think of the proficiencies as the ingredients of the performance base recipe. By themselves, ingredients have no chance of becoming a beautiful culinary delight. They need a set of methods and practices that will turn them into a dish that tastes great. You may have 10 different chefs make a beautiful dish out of the same ingredients, but each dish will taste very different. It is the same with leadership. Like a chef, you need a set of methods and practices to turn the proficiencies into a meaningful whole. Each leader creates a different outcome with the same proficiencies, depending on the leader's style and personality. Just as the amount of heat used, time spent and extra pinches of spice or seasoning is individual to each chef, so, too, is each leader's use of the *social proficiencies*.

If the performance base is the "what" and "why" of our work, then the social proficiencies are the "how". This is where the emotional and social intelligence skills of high-performing leaders come to the fore. It is exciting, and it is an endless journey of improvement and discovery that we all can undertake. The great thing about the social proficiencies is they give us a clearly defined parameter to pour our efforts into, to get first-class performance out of the people around us and increase the quality of the work we do. A leader must be able to inspire, motivate, guide and protect their people. They must grow the people within their sphere.

We are trying to get ourselves and our people into a state of flow, where productivity is off the charts compared to the norm. We are trying to make this repeatable, like being in a constant state of autopilot.

By definition, a leader must have influence over the environment around them. But how?

Not only are we trying to achieve, but we are trying to lead with rhythm and ensure ROE is super high. We are trying to get ourselves and our people into a state of flow, where productivity is off the charts compared to the norm. We are trying to make this repeatable, like being in a constant state of autopilot, accelerating progress and maintaining momentum. To be in synchronisation with each other and our external stakeholders is our destination.

Steven Kotler, founder of the Flow Genome Project and author of *The Rise of Superman*, tells us that when we are in flow, our brains experience a unique cocktail of five hormones: norepinephrine, dopamine, endorphins, anandamide and serotonin. This creates a mental environment where the pain is shut out, focus is heightened to the point that distractions no longer disturb us, and lateral thinking to connect the dots all happen simultaneously. All the while, happy hormones float around our system, giving us a great sense of enjoyment, closeness and connectedness with our teammates.

As leaders, our goal is to achieve this for ourselves, then create an environment where our people experience this all the time. Not asking for much, are we?! It is daunting, and it is a good reason why high-achieving professionals seem to be on an endless pilgrimage of self-help books, courses and podcasts (myself included). After studying such topics, I have concluded that all this can be approached by focusing on three pillars of social proficiency that are essential for all leaders and will bring our performance base alive:

1.   **Humility.** Often misunderstood and under-utilised. When leaders harness the power of humility, they create an influence and inspiration that cannot be matched by any form of charisma, natural talent or privilege. Leading from a position of self-importance or popularity pales in comparison to humble leaders, who are infinitely more powerful and impactful in creating positive change and boosting overall team performance.

2. **Audacity.** Often the biggest surprise and looked upon as frivolous or troublesome. When leaders know how to be naughty in the right ways and set their thinking apart from others, they become a beacon of hope, aspiration and motivation. Teams led by audacious leaders stand taller, think deeply and create more.

3. **Tenacity.** Often known but not practised to the extent required. The ability to not give up, especially in the toughest moments, is essential if leaders are to keep the troops believing and pushing beyond their mental barriers, as well as the inhibiting forces all businesses experience. Teams with tenacious leaders are the toughest, tightest and most likely to turn into high-performing units.

Affectionately called the *HAT competencies*, these three pillars of the social proficiencies create an environment of continual uplift in commitment, courage and confidence. By instilling these three Cs in ourselves and our people, we clear a distinct pathway towards autonomy, belonging and eventual mastery for all concerned. Once we implement this process, we can rinse and repeat for bigger challenges across a wider influence (rhythm).

As intimated above, the HAT competencies of the rhythm building blocks link with the performance base. The social proficiencies create a positive and continual feedback loop with the analytical proficiencies. We can hold the space to continually refine and update the "why" of our work. This is known as *performance feedback*. It is the ability of a leader to zoom in on an action or person at a granular level, while also being able to zoom out to an overall strategic plan. The social proficiencies give a leader the ability to take the 5xM Framework and work it in multiple dimensions, with open dialogue that creates inclusion and a culture of learning.

The HAT competencies are also a powerful way to leverage the technical skills of oneself and the team. When a leader uses the HAT competencies consistently, the technical skills are activated in an extremely productive and efficient manner – not only in volume but also in quality. Decision making is clearer and, therefore, of a higher quality. Achievement begets achievement to create a tangible momentum that can be seen and measured.

This is what makes rhythm such a robust and captivating way of working. Not only do we have the skills to be brilliant, but we can implement them at the right moments calmly and accurately. In sporting terms, this is called *clutch*: the basketball player who can make the shot in the last second to win the match; the cricket bowler who can bowl "in the death" at the end of an innings; or the swimmer who can relax and perform their strategy in the Olympic final. It is the opposite of *choke*, when a player buckles under pressure and experiences panic, tension and doubt – the inhibitors of rhythm and the antithesis of what we are trying to achieve as leaders.

This is why the interlink between the HAT competencies and the technical proficiencies creates *performance execution*. The competencies and proficiencies take our workplace-equivalent ingredients and animate them with good, solid decision making and action in the face of constantly changing environments, competing priorities and hundreds of unique human interactions every day. The game of ROE is based on the constant cycle of improvement between these three building blocks of technical, analytical and social proficiencies. Firstly, we learn them; then we practise them. By practising them, we develop our ability to be autonomous. If we do this for long enough, we gain mastery in our role. With this level of ability, we find rhythm easily and get into rhythm often enough where we master our post. We create an environment where our teams can practise, become autonomous and find mastery themselves. Then we progress, find new challenges and elevate ourselves to the next level. The progress is endless.

CHAPTER 6

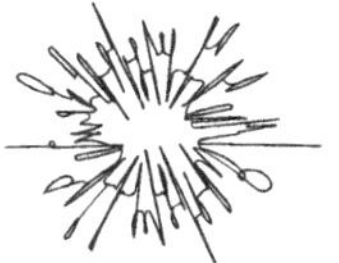

Bringing the Base Alive

"Collective intelligence is not that different in some ways than apes in a forest. One ape is enthusiastic, and that signal recruits others, and they jump in and start doing some stuff together. That's the way group intelligence works, and this is what people don't get. Just hearing something said rarely results in a change of behaviour. They're just words. When we see people in our peer group play with an idea, our behaviour changes. That's how intelligence is created. That's how culture is created."
– Alex "Sandy" Pentland, MIT

The Only HAT You'll Ever Need

I have always believed that emotional intelligence (EQ) is a major part of performance and an even bigger factor in leadership. This was confirmed when I went through my ESCI (Emotional and Social Competency Inventory) accreditation with the Hay Group consulting firm. In the first exercise, we were asked to think of the worst boss we had ever had and list the things they did that made them so poor. Then we were asked to envisage the best boss we had ever had and list their attributes. From everything that was written, the majority of behaviours and traits had something to do with relationship management and self-management (the social proficiencies in Chapter 5).

Bad bosses tended to be inaccessible and difficult to approach. They could be overbearing, sometimes publicly berating and belittling staff. They were generally inconsistent in their messaging and focused on political manoeuvring to progress their career. The good bosses were characterised as knowing their stuff and having good business acumen, but the list was dominated by things like humour, honesty, a growth mindset, vulnerability, curiosity, the ability to flex to the needs of other people, and disciplined. We have all experienced working under both types of leader. I am sure most of us would recognise such leaders within a short time of working under them. It is easy to feel, but it is difficult to pinpoint exactly how a good manager does what they do. And it can be difficult to know where a bad manager needs to start if they want to improve.

Knowing that social competency is an essential part of leadership is the first step to acknowledging the pathway to excellence. The self-management and relationship management required to align with and continually improve business is essential. The myth that a great leader needs to be a brilliant orator or a naturally charismatic and charming personality must be squashed. I believe this "standard" is not helpful (nor is it true!), and it is intimidating for everyday people who are graduating in their profession, getting some runs on the board, and being promoted to leadership positions. Do we need to suddenly be amazing speakers like Winston Churchill or Martin Luther King, Jr? Do we need to be supremely heroic like the characters in an *Avengers* movie? Or do we need to be hardnosed and scrupulous like Steve Jobs or Gina Rinehart?

The good news is we can dump these myths for good. When leaders have a good performance base, the HAT competencies (introduced in Chapter 5 and explained further here) become the biggest priority. They can help any leader understand how to behave (and think) as a leader who wants to be good at what they do (i.e. lead a highly synchronised team).

The HAT competencies

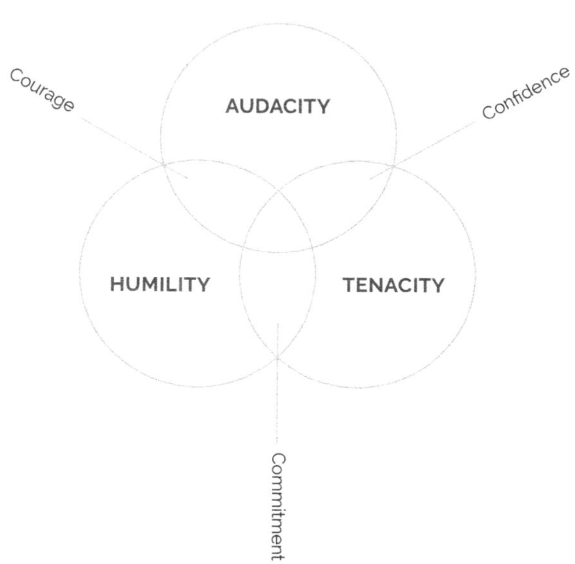

The HAT competencies have a few rules:

1. They Are 100% Implementable by Everyone in Their Own Unique Way

There are no scripts, and they are not exclusive to any personality type or learning style. They can be crafted, developed and expressed in whatever manner is relevant to you and your environment. For leaders in big businesses, they help you extract the best bits of a company's culture and snuff out the friction-filled poor behaviours in and around your team. For leaders in small businesses, they help you guide and grow the business through slim cash-flow scenarios and hustle-oriented cultures. Leaders taking over a team in the extinction phase or synchronisation phase will use the HAT competencies to obtain and sustain their own rhythm and improve performance as they face new and dynamic challenges.

2. They Are All Equal

No competency is more important than the others. They all need time, energy and focus. There is no pecking order, and they are lesser without each other, too, as they either ground or energise each other. All are essential to creating rhythm for oneself and a team. Should one competency be left behind, the whole framework breaks down.

3. They Are Not Equal

Every one of us is naturally in tune with some of these competencies more than others. As you read about them, you will reflect on which ones you may already execute at a high standard. Others will be foreign or underdeveloped, and some will be more relevant to your current challenges than the rest. So, the emphasis can be shifted to suit your situation. I will introduce the competencies in the natural order for learning, but you can apply them in a unique and specific way that suits your needs (and that of your people). I help leaders define this within the Rhythm Effect diagnostics and programs.

Being an expert in the HAT competencies generates an endless power bank of influence, enabling a leader to create truly exceptional synchronisation within their team. Once this is achieved, the team will never be the same again.

Humility – The Cornerstone

"Thank you" is such a simple phrase. Yet in one moment, these two words became the most influential story of the 2018 Football World Cup. The Japanese team was eliminated in a very cruel way in the round of 16 against Belgium in Rostov, Russia. The winner would go through to the quarter finals, an achievement the Japanese team had failed to do in its entire history. Japan's national team, affectionately known as the "Samurai Blue", was the last Asian Confederation team left in the competition. Even though it was ranked 67 in the world at the time, it was an in-form team and scored the first two goals of the game against the highly fancied Belgians. It was looking like Japan would finally progress to become the most successful Japanese team in World Cup history.

But with the last kick of the game, Belgian striker Nacer Chadli scored to break Japanese hearts, capping off a three-goal second half. In an instant, Japan was knocked out 3–2. At such a moment, professional sportspeople tend to cry, slump and become aggravated. In world football, an industry where teams are full of multi-millionaires under the age of 30, professional and decent behaviour can be uncommon. Players sometimes leave the field without acknowledging the opposition or their fans. Throwing drink bottles and shouting expletives are commonplace. And always, no matter the result or circumstance, the change rooms are left in a filthy state, with mud, strapping, bottles and all sorts of rubbish strewn over the floor, lockers and showers.

Yet in this moment of despair, the Japanese team took the time at the end of the game to bow to the crowd. The players went back to the dressing room quietly and without fuss. They got changed and left the stadium – but not before cleaning their change room to an immaculate standard. It was spotless. To top this off, they left a note written in the Russian alphabet saying, "Spasibo" – thank you. At the same time, the Japanese spectators were photographed with plastic bags in their hands, cleaning the stadium while they cried about their team's loss.[47] [48] For a culture that prides itself on order, cleanliness and respect, this was a step further than anyone would have expected. An act of pure class.

The game had given the sporting world a spectacle of excitement and goals; everything you would want from a World Cup football match. Yet the biggest story was how these players and fans cleaned up after themselves. They showed great humility and respect to their hosts and the property. The gesture was as shocking as it was nice. But why does such an act of humility gain headlines around the world? Why do acts of humility like this have such a powerful effect on us? And, on top of this, why does a humble person or group inspire us to do and be better?

These are important questions to keep in mind when we lead. But to answer them fully, we need to understand what humility is.

In the ancient worlds of Vikings and the Roman Empire, societies operated on an honour versus shame value system. The best thing someone could hope for was to come from a proud and strong family, which was why people would introduce themselves as the son of their father and grandfather. To be of a noble family or house was honourable, and honour was more important than anything, including money and health. To bring shame on the family name was the worst thing you could do. If you were of equal status to someone, you would never humble yourself to them. Taking any action that would position you as subservient would be a disgrace to yourself and your entire family. It was only acceptable to humble yourself to people of royalty or the gods. Often, this would come in the form of bowing to them, fighting for them or giving service to them (i.e. some sort of sacrifice).[49]

From these ancient traditions and ways of thinking, the idea of humility was born. To be "beneath" someone else was, to some extent, regarded as humiliating. Even in an unspoken way, if there was a hierarchy and I was figuratively serving you, then it would mean you were more important and powerful than me, and my worth would be understood in these terms. Therefore, if I was in a position of power and degraded myself or stooped to the level of the people below me, this would be a way to humiliate myself. It is a perspective we need to be aware of, as serving others is, in fact, a position of power and influence. To be humble and utilise humility is a critical leadership trait that is very different to humiliating oneself.

We no longer live in an ancient world, and the value system of our society has shifted. Today's Western societies generally rotate around the ideals of good and evil. We are interested more in the creation of pleasure and the reduction of suffering, and prosperity has become the north of our compass, which opposes poverty. These values mean you can come from any class or background and become a modern-day king – something unthinkable in an ancient society. Oprah Winfrey was born into poverty and is now the most recognised woman on international television, with a personal wealth of approximately $3 billion. Ralph Lauren grew up in modest circumstances and worked as a clerk before building his clothing empire. And steel tycoon Lakshmi Mittal was born into a low-income family in Rajasthan and now runs the world's largest steel-making company.[50]

Such people are held as examples of great accomplishment in modern society. They are role models for younger generations, representing prosperity, goodness and pleasure. Ironically, their value is derived from the sheer volume of people they serve. Their influence is almost entirely reliant on the products they produce being of value to the people who consume them. Winfrey provides enjoyment, entertainment and pleasure to millions of people around the world. She works tirelessly to speak to these people and ensures they get every bit of pleasure from her wide array of publications and productions. Likewise, Lauren knows that every collection needs to inspire and wow the high expectations of the fashion industry and the general public – otherwise, they won't buy the products.

When put in such simple terms, it is easy to see that serving others is critical if we want to become influential or, at the very least, influence other people's performance. But this central concept seems to get lost in an old-world view of leadership. If we, as leaders, display acts of humility and serve others in this powerful way, we can inspire others to serve more, give more of themselves, and commit to the common cause the team is trying to achieve (commitment is enhanced).

In all my research, the characteristic of humility is the one that continually pops up. Jim Collins states that humility is what separates the level 5 leaders (the cream of the crop) from the rest (as we touched on in Chapter 4). In his bestselling book, *Leaders Eat Last*,[51] Simon Sinek cites an array of business and military leaders who displayed humility to lead amazing teams that performed better than any other. And it is humility that is the basis of *servant leadership*, fathered by Robert K. Greenleaf in 1977.

The common denominator is this: when people see a leader thinking of others before themselves, it is inspiring. Team members stress and worry less because they feel safe, can work freely, and can be comfortably vulnerable with the team (courage is enhanced). When leaders act on self-interests only, it is dispiriting and detrimental to team performance – like when a boss takes credit for someone else's work. It makes us vomit a little. Or when a boss applies pressure on their team to hit numbers just so he or she can achieve a bonus and look good at the next company conference. Yuck! If this is commonplace and people are not inspired to perform, sooner or later, they will leave, and they will perform poorly in the meantime. Elements of resentment, politics and general unrest tend to fester in such an environment, which grows into an unhappy, toxic and counter-productive culture.

Yet if we can learn how to harness our humility as leaders, our power to create a high-performing team and organisation drastically increases. In my experience, many people are humble in their intention as leaders but find humility difficult to express or leverage as a leadership trait.

The following three competencies are great ways of building humility as a leadership performance trait, which will remove friction from your workflow, increase calm and relaxation in your thinking, and help the team similarly, allowing rhythm to develop.

Building Humility

1. Comms That Count

It's not about you. You probably know this but let me be severely clear – *it is not about you!* I am so forceful about this because it is a foundational principle of leadership that is often broken. In an age where everyone owns their own media channel (social media) and is building their personal brand, it is difficult not to break this principle and make it "all about me". But, as leaders, break it we must not! When the messaging, the work or the outcomes are about the leader, it is a step towards becoming the office jerk. More importantly, it is a step towards losing the team and their commitment to the job – something none of us can afford. It is a sure way to extinction.

This plays out in our communications. A leader needs to motivate, inspire and guide their team. So, when it comes to communication, what is the best way to do this? Communication is not confined to the big, rousing speeches at conferences or meetings. These moments can be useful, but they do not inspire high-performing teams as much as we assume they do. It's the small, private moments that make the difference.

All too often, leaders deliver their big ideas and are not seen again. When urgent problems arise, they go missing. They cannot be found. They are in their ivory tower, hiding in an office or behind their email, or on holiday. A public example of this was when the Prime Minister of Australia, Scott Morrison, was on holiday in Hawaii while his country was literally on fire.[52] More than 12.6 million hectares burned in the biggest wildfires ever recorded in Australia. Thirty-three people died, more than a billion animals lost their lives, and it is estimated that 10.6 million Australians were worried about their safety or that of a loved one.[53] The country was under siege by this natural disaster, but its leader did not jump on a plane to engage with the problem. He left it to his assistant until public pressure rose so steeply that he had no choice.

Why did the public get so upset about this? Why did it matter so much? Logically, his presence probably didn't make too much difference, as there was a competent chain of command doing a great job at the time. If anything, Morrison's presence could have distracted the experts in charge of the situation. The answer is in our basic emotional need to feel safe, which has little to do with logic. A leader is responsible for upholding and promoting safety. If they don't, doubts grow (the antithesis of rhythm). In this case, Morrison's job was not only to communicate safety and support in his speech but, more importantly, to show them in his actions. This is no different to what is required of any leader in any of our workplaces.

The best way for a leader to show support and signal safety is in the small, private moments. Belonging is a basic human need and, when we feel it strongly, we tend to be more relaxed and able to perform. Alex "Sandy" Pentland has researched human behaviours more than almost anyone else in the world. He and his team at MIT coined the term *belonging cues*. These are animated communications that make people feel safe, secure and included.[54] Pentland gives the following examples of belonging cues:

- **Over-communicate your listening.** Be present and animate your listening with lots of "mms" and "ahs", and ask follow-up questions. This shows you are actively listening and in the moment with the other person, displaying a strong sense of care.

- **Show your imperfections.** Forget trying to be perfect or having all the answers. We need to maintain our credibility with our team, but asking people to help fill in the gaps is a powerful way of telling others that they matter and their opinion is valued. Admitting when you get things wrong also lowers everyone's guard and allows for freer and more open communication.

- **Embrace the messenger.** The worse the news, the more important it is to show love and support to the person who spoke up and raised the issue. This promotes courage and trust in ways no team-building weekend away or Friday drinks ever could.

- **Over-communicate your thank yous.** Recognising people's efforts lifts their motivation. It shows people you are watching and registering their efforts, even when the results are not good. Think Samurai Blue! This signals to everyone loud and clear that you are across the business and can see the hard work and effort people are putting in, which motivates more of the same behaviour.

The effect of meaningful communications is maximised when done often in private as opposed to occasionally in public. A leader does not limit their social proficiencies to only their direct reports. So, have one on ones with team members, peers and superiors. The powerful effect of *"comms that count"* comes to the fore and compounds when a leader quietly talks with people constantly.

As leaders, we need to speak to our people a lot. Quantity is just as important as quality. A quiet word of encouragement. A quiet word of guidance. A quiet word of support. A quiet word of discipline. All for one reason: it will serve the person you are speaking to. It will make them better, clearer and more energised. It has nothing to do with you.

The big speeches are always going to be a part of a leader's job, but they are not as important as we think. In fact, charisma and charm are overrated when it comes to leadership. They help, but to be a great leader, we do not need to be wordsmiths or extroverts. We need to care deeply and show this every day in our consistent communication, delivered in an individualistic way to suit the people we work with.

2. Emotional Control

As leaders, we are constantly faced with big and small problems. Every time a problem is solved and we get some clear air, another fire comes at us that needs putting out. It can be draining, frustrating and make rhythm impossible to achieve. Especially when people do daft stuff – it is infuriating! A senseless mistake or action made by a client or staff member can create a big mess, and guess who has to clean it up? The leader. It is a guarantee of leadership, and how we manage these scenarios can define how long we last and how the business tracks during our tenure. As a fiery Italian, this has always been a struggle for me. I tend to show my emotions easily and regularly. If I am pissed off, you'll probably know by how I walk into the room!

In my various leadership positions, when things were going bad or mistakes were made, I always struggled to maintain a positive and consistent persona. I was a bit up and down. It took me many years to figure out how much my lack of *emotional control* undermined all the hard work I was doing, as well as what my teams were doing. The worst thing was that I knew better from what I had learnt playing high-level cricket.

As a bowler, I was taught to remain steady. If you get hit around by the batsman, you cannot afford to drop your head. You need to keep level headed, formulate and reassess your plans, then execute. Conversely, when things go well and you take lots of wickets, you cannot get over-excited or start celebrating too early. An inkling of complacency is all it takes for opposition teams to take back ascendancy and create real problems for a bowler. The aim of the game is to remain steady minded no matter what – constant and unshakable. And it is the same for leaders in any business.

When a leader loses their rag (gets impatient or angry), it sends a signal that they have lost control and the team is in trouble. It is not going to enhance focus, execution or performance in any shape or form. I learnt this from a good friend of mine, Dean Yasharian. When I met Dean, he was the executive chef of Bar Boulud at the Mandarin Oriental, London, before he moved back to his native USA as the head chef at the famous Chateau Marmont in West Hollywood. He now has his own restaurant, Perle, in Pasadena, California. I remember him saying to me, *"When a chef gets angry in the kitchen, he has lost control of service."* I was fortunate to watch Dean work with his crew on a few occasions and see how he handled mini disasters in the kitchen. This big, burly bloke would quietly and seamlessly swoop in to support stations that were struggling. If he needed to take over a station and relieve someone so they could take a breather, he did. Or he would direct a line cook who was struggling in a way no one would have noticed unless you were watching like a hawk (i.e. like I was!). Yet the most important thing he did in these situations was to remain calm. He stayed centred and did not blow a gasket or humiliate the underperforming person.

The All Blacks (New Zealand's national rugby team) call this "keeping a blue head" – to maintain a cool demeanour and thought pattern.[55] Like fire, when our mind turns red, hot and agitated, we can become unpredictable, destructive and sporadic. Good decisions and effective communication are near impossible. Keeping our minds blue during times of stress and adversity has a direct correlation with building humility. When we turn red, we tend to be in a state of catastrophe.

When we catastrophise, we say things like:

- *"Why does this always happen to me?"*
- *"Can we have one day when things actually work around here?!"*
- *"Why am I the one who always has to clean up the mess?"*
- *"Nothing ever goes smoothly around here!"*

There are some constants in such catastrophic rhetoric. Firstly, the above statements deal in absolutes. Terms like "always" and "never" are not the truth in most circumstances. Secondly, they emphasise the impact on the individual or self – the focus is on "me". There is an element of victimisation, a trait that does not serve a leader well. In fact, these statements are the opposite of humility because the leader is thinking of themselves before those around them. Their intention may be good, in the sense that they care deeply about doing good work or achieving good results, but this victim talk is more about themselves than the people they lead (or serve). Ultimately, these responses add more fiction to proceedings, creating more tension, more work and a bigger chance of division and derision.

By mastering the ability to keep a blue head instead of turning red, a leader demonstrates leadership humility. They stay in the zone of service and, therefore, keep the task or project on track. Emotional control is, in fact, a courageous act that promotes courage in those around you. The leader works in problem-solving mode, making the situation better for all stakeholders. It also sends a clear signal of support, assuredness and safety – everything the humble leader aims to achieve. By keeping our emotions under control, we regain or continue being in rhythm. It is more powerful than many of us will ever realise. And a leader with a blue head is certainly the type of leader we all want by our side when true catastrophe hits.

3. No Thanks

We talk a lot about the importance of workplace culture in our modern organisations. It may be onsite, in-store or in an office. Whatever your context, two places tell me almost everything I need to know about how a team is tracking from a cultural point of view: the toilets and lunchroom. An overflowing rubbish bin in the kitchen is a telling sign. The big one is toilet paper. Is there spare toilet paper ready to go? And, more importantly, do people replace the roll when it runs out? For me, this is a window into the mentality of the team. As an outsider, these signals are like loud air horns sounding out, *"Warning! Warning!"* They tend to become normalised and, therefore, non-existent to the people who work there. They can be seen as meaningless minor elements of a business, but I couldn't disagree more. It's the small token gestures that bind and tighten a team or destroy it if they don't happen. These seemingly small acts are loud signals that give us insight into how people treat each other and their work. They reveal the team's mentality.

As a leader, how can you encourage your team to show more care for each other and the company's assets? How can you enhance the respect people have for each other and the job at hand?

Merely telling people to do something is one of the most ineffective ways to create behavioural change, yet it tends to be our default. For generations, we have been telling kids not to take drugs. They know it is bad for them, yet many still do it. No matter how much the parental generations repeat how bad drugs are, no matter the punishments, the results stay the same. Sometimes, they're even worse! Authoritative leadership does not work.

So, what does work?

Role modelling. Showing is one of the most powerful leadership activities we can undertake. Even more powerful is when the highest-ranked person in the team is happy to do the dirty work, especially to help someone else. When Chris Coleman, former manager of Sunderland Football Club, picked up a shovel in the middle of winter to shovel snow off the pitch, so the players had a surface to train on, the office staff soon jumped in to help.[56] It showed the players how important it was that everyone mucked in and that everyone was willing to do whatever it took to win. These are acts of love. They're powerful. Recognition and reward are not at the heart of these leadership acts – they are thankless. And the more leaders do these acts, the more others will proactively do them, too. It sets a standard that bleeds into other areas of work. People feel cared for, and a reciprocity loop begins.

Former CEO of the McDonald's Corporation, Fred Turner, was the right-hand man to Ray Kroc. Kroc was the man who took an idea from the McDonalds brothers and turned it into a global franchise juggernaut. Turner was once quoted as saying about Kroc:

> *"Every night, you'd see him coming down the street, walking close to the gutter, picking up every McDonald's wrapper and cup along the way. He'd come into the store with both hands full of cups and wrappers. I saw Ray spend one Saturday morning with a toothbrush cleaning out holes in the mop wringer. No one else really paid attention to the damned mop wringer, because everyone knew it was just a mop bucket. But Kroc saw all the crud building up in the holes, and he wanted to clean them so the wringer would work better."*[57]

It is a clear signal that the leader has no professional narcissism whatsoever. He is willing to do whatever it takes for everyone to be successful and for the collective to be successful. It also signals that no one is too big to do whatever needs to get done. The message is clear: *"If you do not care to this level, then maybe you should not be here."* It is this essential principle that means these acts do not become sources of resentment, where one feels like they are the "dog's body" or "lacky" for the rest of the team. When the leader works longer and harder than everyone else, then picks up the trash, too, this can cause real anger and frustration for the leader. But remember, these are acts of care. They display the standards of behaviour you want to see in others – that's where the power comes from. When you role model desired behaviours and discuss with your team why they are important (which the analytical proficiencies assist with), you will see dramatic behavioural change based on commitment thinking or "team first" thinking instead of a "me first" mentality.

Mahatma Gandhi once said, *"Find yourself in the service of others."* As leaders, we can enjoy these moments. We can learn a lot from them, and it can be enjoyable to do something that makes someone else's life better. In times of crisis, this is also a great way to alleviate anxiety. A client of mine was under tremendous pressure when COVID-19 hit in March 2020. He utilised the idea of *"no thanks"* in his daily mindset and actions to ensure others around him had everything they needed. He remarked to me, *"I was so consumed with making sure everyone else was taken care of, I had no room to feel stressed myself."* A shift in culture is created from this humble way of working. Rather than doing something "because I have to", people do selfless acts because they want to. It becomes contagious and is a quick win so leaders can improve team momentum, cohesion and a sense of belonging.

When considered a cultural pillar, this humble way of leading and working reduces all sorts of friction and enhances synchronisation in multiple ways. The power of such humility in a leader not only makes a big difference to the practical tasks that need to get done, but everyone serves each other so much more effectively, creating a basis for uninterrupted trust. If rhythm is missing in your team, then this lever of humility is the first that needs to be pulled. The smoothness of how a team operates will elevate substantially, making work more enjoyable, profitable and resilient.

Audacity – The Surprise

When we join a company, we usually receive a code of conduct handbook. We may even get a "welcome pack" with stories about the founder and insights into the company's culture, as well as a policy and procedure (P&P) manual. These handbooks and P&P manuals give us a standard to which the company expects us to behave, which we can all agree is a good thing. But in most corporate environments, these manuals read as one big, fat rule book. The underlying message is: *"You will do all of this or else!"*

Control and standardisation are important when there is a large number of employees, and, in general, people tend to conform. But what if none of these rules was spelled out? What if there were no rules? Would there be anarchy? Possibly. But one successful American business has bucked the trend with its employee handbook, which consists of one rule. Nordstrom was started in 1901 by John W. Nordstrom, a Swedish immigrant, and his partner, Carl F. Wallin, in Seattle, USA.[58] This small shoe shop would expand into one of the most successful department store brands in the US. It has consistently outperformed its rivals for decades.[59] A Nordstrom family member still sits at the top of the business today, and, along with its savvy business acumen, the company is held as a shining example of how culture can form the backbone of great results. Nordstrom's one rule epitomises this. The company's handbook is famous for being a simple 5x8" grey card with the following words on it:

Welcome to Nordstrom

We're glad to have you with our Company. Our number one goal is to provide outstanding customer service. Set both your personal and professional goals high. We have great confidence in your ability to achieve them.

Nordstrom Rules: Rule #1: Use best judgment in all situations. There will be no additional rules.

Please feel free to ask your department manager, store manager or division general manager any question at any time.[60]

It sends a clear message to the employees: we trust you and want you to be autonomous. More importantly, it sends a clear signal to everyone that they should treat the business as if it was their own. To be a mere employee who is only there to follow orders is a limited brief for anyone's work. It is one of the biggest restraints to business performance I have observed over my 15 years of consultancy. If we can get our people to think for themselves and problem solve without needing to defer to superiors, then the whole experience for everyone will be enhanced.

This free-spirited approach to business and management can seem counterintuitive. In a world that requires us to follow the rules and think procedurally, it seems weird that one of the key social proficiencies is to be *audacious* – to experiment, think freely and sometimes go against the grain. But without audacity, it is near impossible to gain rhythm. The reason is that a rules-laden environment makes a complex world even more complex. Layers of bureaucracy are added. More metrics, more reports and more stakeholders. They create friction.

Yves Morieux is a world-leading corporate transformation expert and the director of Boston Consulting Group's Institute of Organisation. His findings tell us that lots of rules mean employees are not incentivised to cooperate or collaborate. But they are incentivised to hit KPIs, even if it is at the cost of progress. The result is a startling fall in overall productivity and effectiveness. As Morieux says, *"Our organisations are wasting human intelligence. They have turned against human efforts. When people don't cooperate, don't blame their mindsets, their mentalities, their personality – look at the work situations."*[61]

Like the chef who cooks with their soul or the guitarist who plays a riff like no one else, there is an ascendancy of spirit and outcome that cannot be obtained without dare and freedom. Without audacity, we are unable to create or lead creative teams. And please, be under no illusion – creating and doing new things that have never been done before is part of the definition of high-performing teams. Mediocre teams focus on what has been done rather than creating a new future. When "keeping hold of what we have" is the dominant mindset, as opposed to thinking about the "possibilities we could achieve", there is a tension that creates more problems than it solves. Guarding what we have and conforming as a default leads us to a place of restriction and protectionism. As a leader, it is easy to see that this is not a good environment for flow and ongoing rhythm.

The real power of audacity (like all the HAT competencies) is in role modelling. It is uplifting when the team sees a leader smile and give a quiet wink before taking on a scary or overwhelming situation. When people see their leader put themselves at risk for everyone else's benefit, it is inspiring. When the leader comes out the other side with a good result and unharmed, they are once again inspired. They register these events and are encouraged to "think differently", as the old Apple computers slogan once said. Team members feel less scared of obstacles and less daunted to take on bigger challenges (courage is enhanced). Along with this, team members find themselves believing that new possibilities are achievable. The leader has shown everyone that what had seemed impossible is truly possible. The old imaginary rules they operated under via their assumptions are shattered. All of a sudden, the collective mentality is we can do this. I can do this. I can really do it! There is a belief that was not there before (confidence is enhanced).

When I used to see naughty kids in the school playground, I wrote them off as brats. Now, I see future leaders. They have a natural ability to see the possibilities and are not afraid to see what happens if they try something outside the rules. For some of us, this does not come naturally. We need to find our own style and strengthen our audacity using the competencies explained below.

Audacity is not the first thing we think about when it comes to performance and leadership, but it is essential. There is no rhythm if we are in a fixed and rigid state. Audacity can bind teams and is central to one's ability to achieve outcomes they may not have dreamt of previously. Audacious leaders make the impossible feel possible to all on the journey.

Building Audacity

1. Break the Rules

"Who wrote the rule..." has got to be one of my all-time favourite sayings. It is a mantra I am sure many people use, but I was first introduced to it by Danny Meyer in his book, *Setting The Table*.[62] It speaks to the flawed idea that many of us operate under: we assume the world has a board of directors who set the rules. Meyer used this question of "who wrote the

rule" to ask why couldn't it be possible to serve classic fine-dining Italian or French cuisine in a relaxed, accommodating setting that leveraged "American friendliness and hospitality". Up until that point in the 1980s, if you wanted a classic European culinary experience in New York, you had to go to a place where men needed to wear sports coats, and the waiters wore a black tie and white gloves. An elitist environment if ever there was one. Meyer ripped up the rule book and carved out a niche in the New York City restaurant industry, where diners experienced first-class food in a warm and friendly environment.

A world of opportunity opens for all of us when we start scrutinising the assumptions that distract us or hold us back. It is fascinating to see how many imaginary rules we operate under. Sometimes they are personal:

- *"I am not good enough to achieve that."*
- *"I don't deserve to have that."*
- *"No matter how hard I work, I could never achieve that."*

Sometimes they are organisational:

- *"We are a small player and could never compete with the big boys."*
- *"We don't have the talent or resources to be successful."*
- *"Those targets global management have given us are impossible to achieve!"*

When I run sessions with teams and leaders in corporate environments, we uncover the often unspoken and unwritten rules everyone operates under. It is astounding and transformative. The negative and crippling effect these imaginary rules have on people's performance is sizable. The side effect is that the organisation's reputation and profitability suffer. In one session, a national manager had no idea that the team felt like they couldn't give feedback to the executives. It was an eye opener for everyone and freed the business in multiple ways, opening opportunities for rhythm everywhere.

Breaking the rules has nothing to do with breaking compliance or doing anything illegal. It is about questioning assumptions, pushing boundaries and finding new, improved ways of doing things. It is open to everyone, and freedom and belief wait on the other side. Leaders not only garner closeness and cohesion by breaking the rules on behalf of a team, but they also promote an environment where rule breaking is encouraged by team members.

Harvard professor, author of *Rebel Talent* and a world-leading expert in rule breaking Francesca Gino states eight key ways to break the rules:

1. **Break routine.** Purposefully break routine to shake things up. I saw the Sydney Sixers women's Big Bash cricket team run an egg-and-spoon race as part of their warm-up before a game on the Sydney Cricket Ground. It was a serious match, and they are a serious team. But this was a great way to inject some fun into their routine. Warm-up drills are mundane, yet the cricketers in this team were having the time of their lives. It was a great way to freshen the atmosphere and create a bonding experience – such a weapon in promoting synchronisation. What is your egg-and-spoon equivalent?

2. **Fish for dissent.** If you are the boss and everyone agrees with you and your entire agenda, you should be worried. And you should be *really* worried if they laugh at all your jokes when you know they are not funny! A lack of diversity in thinking is one of the most dangerous cultural characteristics you can have in your organisation. It will lead to a spiral of poor decisions that creates more work and friction than can be recovered from if it goes on for too long. If people agree with you on a topic, it may be worth asking them why. Getting people's opinion before you give yours is also a good idea. If people feel safe to bring their original ideas, thoughts and experiences to the table, instead of simply consuming information, ticking boxes and mindlessly nodding (think existors!), then rhythm becomes almost inevitable.

3. **Plussing.** Get into the habit of taking a thought or proposal one step further in a non-judgmental way. Instead of saying, *"Yes, but …"* (which is still a valid way to encourage deeper discussion),

say, *"Yes, and …"* to encourage more thought and creativity. It is a wonderful way to test theories and remove limits and assumptions from initial ideas. I use "plussing" to energise discussions that are insipid or flat and to uncover the real reasons why we do a particular action or process. Talk about enhancing clarity!

4. **No masks.** One of my favourite career moments was working with Dean Wallace, salon sales extraordinaire. In Victoria, Australia, almost everyone in the industry knows him (if not nationally!). I had the privilege of working side by side with him for nearly three years. Dean knows his numbers and the industry like the back of his hand and is one of the zaniest people I know. As a salesman, he is phenomenal. He can pivot from joking around with the young assistants on the salon floor to presenting to global executives. Dean understands corporate politics and SME business (his clients). And his favourite saying? *"You can't bullshit a bullshitter!"* This always gets a giggle out of me. But what Dean is really saying here is that people can tell when you are not being you. They can tell if you are pulling a fast one or being disingenuous. Authenticity is a huge topic and one I cannot cover in this text, but sometimes the best rule to break is the one that says you have to act super professional and be someone you are not. It tends to cause more anxiety and stress than anything else and, at the very least, is counterproductive from a leadership point of view. The only way to flow into rhythm is to "do you". As the saying goes, *"Be yourself; everyone else is taken!"*

5. **Never be a slave to mastery.** Striving for perfection for the sake of it is problematic. Defining and refining your technique is important (refer to the technical proficiencies in Chapter 5), but they are a means to an end. Techniques and processes are part of our performance base, but their application (as well as the results) is more important than making them perfect for the sake of being perfect. If processes or standards do not benefit the team or the client, it is important to ask whether they are necessary at all. This is a high-impact exercise, as process for the sake of process is pedantic and a rhythm killer! Repeat the mantra *"speed is our*

friend", which emphasises getting things done rather than waiting for every element to be in place. Getting bogged down in the nitty-gritty can stall us and lead to procrastination and paralysis. The mindset of *"better done than perfect"* is a great way to gain momentum and progress a project.

6. **Find space within constraint.** Some rules will never change or are best not to be broken. Gravity, evaporation, road rules. So, when something cannot be changed, what other opportunities are there within these boundaries? Tax accountants worldwide make a living out of this. Asking *"what can we do?"* instead of focusing on *"what we cannot do"* creates a dialogue that can turn roadblocks into superhighways. International swimming has had a stream of swimwear innovations that have tested the rules without breaking them (but helped break many world records along the way!). Creating and improving aerodynamic equipment in cycling and F1 racing is a full-time job for technical departments, which are charged with breaking from convention without breaking the codes of the ruling bodies. In our business context, we all have space we don't use, which means we miss opportunities to invent and experiment with new strategies. Having fun with the space we do have releases the feel-good hormones associated with flow and gives us a shared purpose (leading to motivation).

7. **Get down and dirty.** Use the idea of "no thanks" in the explicit manner of doing jobs below your pay grade on purpose. Whenever you hear yourself saying, *"But that's not my job,"* ask yourself whether you are simply sticking with a convention to serve yourself or whether there is an opportunity to get back on the tools to help others. Could you listen, observe and learn? Could you spend time with frontline staff to see things with your own eyes? I always encourage top executives and CEOs to spend some time on the front line with their people. They can discover so much, and the troops absolutely love it. One day a quarter or every six months will tell you more than a year's worth of reports ever will. A synchronisation activity if ever there was one.

8. **Leverage accidents.** How often does something terrible happen and we revert to clean-up mode to try to get back to normal as quickly as possible? In our anxiousness to get back on track, we can lose the chance to discover new opportunities and ways of doing things. Francesca Gino cites Toscanini's, an American ice-cream company, as an example of a business that successfully leveraged an accident. Toscanini's accidentally burnt a batch of ice cream, but instead of throwing it away, they packaged it and gave it to customers who loved it and asked for more. The recipe became their bestselling flavour: burnt caramel. What is your burnt caramel equivalent? Have you had a burnt caramel moment but failed to use it as a pathway to discovery or progress?

All of these are ways in which rules can be broken to increase creativity, expression and belief in our people. All are important ingredients for building and improving forward-moving rhythm. Leaders need to bring these elements alive, show others what is possible by using them, and role model these ways of breaking the rules, so they become part of the team's culture.

2. Stand Up

Injustices. They are more destructive than almost anything we can dream of – at least, in terms of our modern organisations and team play. When a person feels jilted by an injustice, they are more likely to become less motivated and disengage. And when we witness injustice to others, the effect is just as powerful (if not more!).

Many of us would have been in a group of friends at school who bullied other kids at one point or another. Usually, the bully and the rest of the group knew it was wrong. But because of social conventions or the desire to fit in, we went along with it. Watching someone else suffer evokes emotions of helplessness, despair and anxiety. The feeling of safety is lowered for everyone involved and, as our parents and teachers have always told us, a bully is just a scared, insecure coward. Even though we know this, as adults, we continue to stand by while bullying, exclusions and inequities happen all around us in our workplaces.

Sometimes, it is a powerful client who is being unreasonable or belittling our staff. Sometimes, it is a senior executive who takes credit for someone else's work. Or it may come in the form of gossip between team members. Whatever way they are expressed, injustices are rampant in our organisations.

As leaders, we have a responsibility to *stand up* to these injustices. Otherwise, all our hard work to gain and increase trust diminishes. In my experience, whenever a business struggles with performance, cliques and political manoeuvres are happening all over the place. When I was involved in a toxic corporate culture, people were publicly berated. A theme of favouritism came from the general manager, and every time there was a senior management meeting, everyone thought the same thing: CYOA (cover your own arse!). It was a matter of saving your skin and trying to get out with minimal professional and emotional bruising. In the process, departments turned on each other and professional friendships were broken beyond repair. It's no wonder our results went from bad to worse.

On reflection, I ask myself why I didn't stand up. I offer excuses, like:

- *"I did my best."*
- *"I did all I could."*
- *"If I stuck my neck out, I would have made things worse."*
- Or my favourite: *"What could I have done?!"*

Deep down, I know I could have done a lot. And when I didn't do much at all to stand up, it meant my team did not feel protected, safe or engaged in the business. They were constantly distracted and probably spent half their time looking for another job. The worst part of this was that other people were seriously affected, more than I was. Like being back at the schoolyard, I was thankful it wasn't me being bullied, but deep down, I felt sick about it. Demotivated doesn't start to cover how I felt at the time.

Whenever there is an injustice in our organisations, it is a calling to all leaders to stand up, no matter how scary and intimidating the situation is or how small and insignificant it may seem. It may be a matter of standing up for yourself when someone is mistreating you, or it may be a case of standing up for a principle, the company, a client or one of your teammates. Like fronting up to a bully, we gain confidence and respect by taking this action. We realise that overcoming injustice is not so difficult, and we can approach future challenges with more speed and vigour. Most importantly, the people around us feel safer because we are there.

Dr Gregory Walton, an associate professor at Stanford University, researches motivation and achievement. He speaks about our human need to seek danger. In fact, a section in our brain called the amygdala is *"obsessed with sensing danger"*.[63] This is why a leader needs to constantly make people feel safe. There is no point in doing anything just once. Knowing this, we can keep an eye out for inequities (which make people feel unsafe) and stand up to them. Not only to snuff out the poor behaviour (which is good for everyone) but also to show the people around you they are in trusted hands and their future is secure with you. It also role models the standard of behaviour you expect from everyone in the team.

When you see others standing up for themselves or each other, you know you are doing something right. When the team is confident enough to stand up to you when you inadvertently create an injustice, you know you are consolidating and on the way to synchronisation (see Chapter 3).

3. Stand Alone

In 1660, King George II had a hair-brained idea. He lived in a time of monarch rule when religion was more powerful than governments. It was a time when the world was flat, and gods had more influence over wars and people's lives (and livelihoods) than any form of science. Yet King George II did a peculiar thing. He patroned an institution that would study and make sense of the natural world. Gresham College received a royal charter, and the Royal Society of London for Improving Natural Knowledge was founded. It was a scientific establishment that would become a base for the brightest minds to experiment, philosophise and discover like no other place in the world. The motto *Nullius in verba* translates into "take nobody's word for it", and it inspired hundreds of discoveries across all disciplines of science in the coming centuries.[64]

Modern archaeology, photography and microbiology were all born at the Royal Society, amongst many other inventions and modalities of science. Sir Isaac Newton, Charles Darwin, Albert Einstein, Dorothy Hodgkin and Stephen Hawking all had works and positions within the institution. The society also elected the first-ever female fellows in 1945. It is a beacon of being different, and it does it very well. It is an institution that has stood apart from conventional thinking and cultural norms since its inception.

Looking back, it seems like the Royal Society was inevitable, as it was just a bunch of geniuses doing what geniuses do. But the reality was very different. In a non-scientific world, the Royal Society had to fight political and cultural forces at every corner. It lived through many wars and was a secret haven for Jewish scholars during World War II. Its audacious spirit lives on today, and the motto continues to drive different thinking and support people willing to pose questions many are afraid to.

Ironically, by doing the difficult things, we enable ourselves to bond, attract and eventually synchronise for better outcomes. In modern business, Apple turned to the hotel model for its inspiration. In 2001, it opened two stores based on this model, which industry experts predicted would fail. Within three years, they had outgrown their competitors, and in 2004, Apple reached $1 billion in annual sales faster than any retailer in history. By 2018, Apple had 506 stores across 25 countries. Not bad for a retail format that had never been tried before. Apple used highly centralised locations with expensive rent and stylish showrooms, hired non-commissioned salespeople and gave free internet to anyone who entered the store – exactly what the majority of retailers were not doing, and the polar opposite of other tech brands. They introduced the "genius bar" concept, where they served advice on hardware and software instead of drinks. Another first for a technology retailer was its *culture of service* mandate.[65]

Competitors that mocked Apple were left with eggs on their face. At the time, these stores were a big risk for Apple, but in retrospect, it all makes so much sense. Is it that clever to do what everyone else is doing? I feel that many leaders worry too much about tasks, deadlines and meetings (i.e. high-friction/low-rhythm activities) when the focus should be on investigating and questioning the consensus. Leaders and their people benefit when they pose abstract and different directions for the team, and then, most importantly, build a business case to ensure these directions have merit. It is a great way to create progress and take your people on an exciting and daring adventure with a flow of its own.

It may feel counterintuitive to do the opposite of what everyone else is doing to build rhythm. You would think it would increase friction and the need to expend more effort to gain a result. But from a leadership view, *standing alone* means taking steps to build our courage and role modelling this for our people. Without courage, we constantly look over our shoulders, filled with hesitation and doubt. The more often you try to be courageous, the easier it becomes, and your discussions and decisions will be of better quality. The practice of standing alone means we are no longer filled with anxiety or fear, and courageous decisions become comfortable. When our teams see us doing this, they become comfortable with such decision making, too. It is a reminder that a leader needs to take their team through a process of consolidation to be able to achieve synchronisation.

Tenacity – The Thread

When the global financial crisis (GFC) hit London, it was noticeable straight away. Many people I knew in advertising immediately lost their jobs. Financial services professionals scrambled to keep their positions, and retail businesses went into administration every week. I was working at the Aveda Institute in London, one of seven locations of excellence for the brand around the world. We could see the effect of the GFC in the sales figures almost immediately.

At the time, we had more than 80 staff from 23 different countries. The spa department was hit the hardest, as massages and beauty treatments were regarded as superfluous discretionary spending by many loyal guests. The salon held its own but struggled to maintain the lofty growth it had been experiencing, and our retail business was receding. People would still buy products, but not as many. Luxury sectors tend to feel economically weak times less so than other parts of the market, as the lower-end sectors rely on slim margins at high volume, leaving little room for further discounting or leaner practices. Luxury, by nature, also targets clientele who are less affected by economic downturns for practical reasons, as well as emotional ones (i.e. keeping up appearances). But in this case, luxury was feeling the pinch, too.

As a management team, we mucked in and did our best, but we were all in agreement that we needed to raise the white flag when it came to hitting company goals. Except for one person: the general manager, Mette Haxthausen. A tall, blonde Danish woman with piercing blue eyes, Mette would constantly bound in and around the whole location. Always smiling and engaging, she simply would not accept that any given goal could not be achieved. In a supportive and encouraging way, Mette would graciously listen to staff's complaints and worries. However, not once did I ever hear her concede "it cannot be done". This fierce leader would always approach a given situation with a mindset of "what can be done?" Carol Dweck would call this a growth mindset.

But what I witnessed was not just a can-do attitude. The complexity of the business and sheer volume of it, along with such high expectations, meant Mette was constantly under attack. In most moments, she was dealing with some kind of disaster. This would be wearing for anyone. It is this constant fatigue that chews up and spits out many of us – high-performance environments are famous for it. Being the best or trying to be the best is a non-stop strain and struggle, and the Aveda London

---

* There is a metric called the "lipstick index", coined by Leonard Lauder, chairman of Estee Lauder Companies Inc., which states that small luxuries, such as lipstick, increase during times of recession. Lauder noticed that luxury cosmetic items increased in sales following the economic downturn after the 911 terrorist attacks in 2001. Many consulting firms argue this indicator is not accurate, but the premise is – people are loyal to their luxury brands and spend money in economically tough times on luxury items that promote status and the appearance of "doing well", even if those luxury items are smaller-ticket items. Read more here: www.investopedia.com/terms/l/lipstickindicator.asp

flagship was no different. Yet Mette was the constant we could rely on. She adapted, flexed, listened and decided. She presented, talked, hosted and served. As a centre of excellence, a continual stream of corporate VIPs came through. The exposure to prying eyes and critique was a stress we all felt, but Mette was calm and assured. Working with her was one of the most influential experiences of my career. Up to that point in my managerial career, I would inevitably find myself massaging truths and positioning events when things were not going well. I made excuses, gave up and focused my energy on how I would explain a problem or poor performance instead of tackling it.

But after working with Mette, I learnt there was another way. To never give in. To never give up. To never raise the white flag. There is tremendous value in trying. If we never stop trying, everything looks and feels a bit different. As a leader, it has a huge effect on the people around you – how they think, how they act and how they move through challenges. I didn't realise how much I was robbing myself and others of opportunities during all those years I had given up on myself and my team. I realised from watching and working with Mette that there is so much to gain from never giving up, even if the eventual result falls short of the target.

When I learnt to keep myself in the game and "hang in there" for longer, I realised a few things:

1. **I can do a lot.** The Navy Seals are famous for using the 40% rule: when your mind tells you to give up, you have only done 40% of what you are capable of doing.[66] It is not scientific, but there is a lot to suggest that we can do a lot more than we initially feel is possible. I am another anecdotal advocate of this idea. Once I was conscious of it, my ability to keep going through the toughest times increased. On the other side was achievement, new experiences and a feeling of self-efficacy. I proved to myself that I wasn't as weak or incapable as I thought I was.

2. **I was operating on assumptions.** The motivational speakers were right all along. It is possible! I can do it! Not to get carried away,

but it became the truth. Previously, when something was tough or hadn't been done before, I didn't think little old me could achieve that goal. I didn't think I could lead my meandering group of misfits to a victory. I believed someone else better, more experienced or more resourced was required. I assumed I could not do it. I was wrong. When I hung in the game, I found myself doing it. Writing this book is a great example. Two years ago, it was an impossible feat for someone like me (a non-academic) to write and publish a book. It is now done.

3. **I was creative.** Through trying, I found myself seeing, doing and learning more. I had more data to lean on and, therefore, I had deeper conversations. In the end, I found myself with more options to throw at problems. By trying for longer, I was trying more solutions. The more I did it, the better the ideas and outcomes. It may have been the execution of a marketing campaign or the delivery of a product launch. By sitting with problems for longer and seeing them through to the end, I became a platform for creative ideas, solutions and implementations. Motivational speaker Matt Church once said, *"Quantity begets quality."* I couldn't agree more.

Angela Duckworth, psychologist and professor of psychology at the University of Pennsylvania, calls this *grit* (we'll hear more about this later). Author Steven Pressfield calls it *stubbornness*. I love both these descriptions, but I call it *tenacity*.

The Cambridge English Dictionary defines tenacity as *"the determination to continue what you are doing."* I like that; it says it all. When I am working on a challenge, I will not give in to any pressures or inhibiting factors. I will unapologetically keep going. It is powerful, and when others see us attacking our work like this (especially when situations are at their darkest), they realise you have no ulterior motive. They know you are willing to sacrifice yourself for them (enhances commitment). Through action, your team can see you will not bow to any difficulty or distraction (enhances confidence). You will press on, and if they come with you, they will be OK. They are safe. Also, your actions tell them that you believe and that they should believe, too. It is not too long before they start believing in themselves, the group and the business more than they ever imagined possible.

Tenacity takes doubt, distraction and hesitation off the table, and rhythm is possible because of it. Tenacity is proven to be an indicator of future success in young people. Duckworth studied the question, *"Why do some children grow up to succeed and others do not?"* Her research found success had nothing to do with genetics, socioeconomic background, race, privilege or the school a child went to. The one thing that made the ultimate difference between those who succeeded and those who did not was, as she terms it, "grit".[67] Grit is the ability to keep going in the face of the seemingly impossible. Injecting grit and tenacity into our approach to work (and that of our leadership) is critical to building rhythm. Rhythm is ongoing and unrelenting. It does not stop. It has low points and slow points, but it does not stop. Moving forward in the darkest and most difficult times ensures rhythm can exist. When we build tenacity within ourselves and our teams, the tough stuff becomes a lot easier, energy expenditure is a lot lower, and the difficult times can even become enjoyable! We remain solid and robust in the face of constant external factors and friction.

Want to be a calm leader when the pressure is on? Then be the most tenacious person you know. Want to have the most committed and confident team possible? Then breed a tenacious team.

Building Tenacity

1. Purpose

Defining and understanding the reason why we should keep going makes an immense impact on our work. This is different from having a mission, which is a broader, bigger-picture statement (covered in the 5xM Framework and the analytical proficiencies in Chapter 5). *Purpose* is more pointed. It is more direct. In fact, it is what gives us direction and is a key ingredient in our ROE game. If our mission is the reason why we are on a journey, then our purpose is the road we choose to take. The core values, mission, vision and identity of our team all pour into one pot to give our vocation's context. When this context is clear, we can define a strong sense of purpose. Unfortunately, many businesses conjure big statements but rarely use them. They become meaningless, and people can find the whole conversation a little tedious. You even may be rolling your eyes at this right now! But do not despair. Even without a completely clear context, we can build and utilise purpose as leaders.

When our purpose is well defined, we have a strong motivation to get up and try again when we have failed. We tend to find things get complex when we have competing priorities, different interpretations and a wide range of problems to solve. Naming our purpose can be difficult to do, but I think it is our number-one go-to when we face complex situations. The tougher the times get, the more powerful our purpose can be. Without a clear purpose that you and your team understand and agree upon, the more you risk creating an environment of high waste instead of high performance.

As an elite leadership consultant and creator of the Harvard Law School Centre, Nikos Mourkogiannis is highly qualified to talk about purpose. In his book, *Purpose: The Starting Point of Great Companies*, Mourkogiannis says, *"Purpose is the difference between good and great, between honourable success and legendary performance, between fifteen minutes of fame and legacy."*[68] This speaks to the role of purpose in our ability to keep going. If we can harness purpose, we will be able to hang in there and push through to the other side of the challenge.

Some useful ways to define purpose for your context:

1. **Find a personal connection to the company values and mission.** What is your take on it? What part of it speaks to you? What makes you feel something? It is rare to find ourselves in an almost cultish state of devotion to our organisations, even if we are the founder. In fact, cultish business cultures come with many problems, such as a lack of diverse thinking, blind rule-following and, in some cases, they become a mechanism to exploit the weak and

vulnerable.[69] Importantly, finding one meaningful thing about the business value proposition, core values or over-arching mission relevant to you is powerful. Encourage your team members to do the same.

2. **Team identity is critical.** By labelling "who we are", we breed the behaviours associated with that label. In his book, *Atomic Habits*, James Clear says identity is a game changer for breaking bad habits and building great ones. Once you have a clear identity, you identify key behaviours required for that identity. It is then easy for us to step into the role of that identity.[70] A simple example may be to label yourself as a non-smoker. What does a non-smoker do? They don't buy cigarettes. They don't smoke cigarettes. They don't stand in smoking areas. They congregate with other non-smokers. It is not even a choice; it is a non-negotiable part of who they are. When others are smoking, the non-smoker can happily remain chatting with their friends while the smoker must scuffle off to sit in isolation. The non-smoker doesn't have to decide if they will have a puff when their mate lights up. The decision is already made.

    What is your team identity? This is a fun exercise because it can be dreamed up and owned by the current team. They can then become the custodians of this unique identity. It can be different from other teams in your department and a shift from the over-arching company context. Think about it in terms of a swimming pool, where the whole company is the pool. Your team identity is your individual lane. Name it and own it!

3. **Discuss purpose at every team meeting.** Update it, adjust it and continually enhance it. If your people find "purpose" a little difficult to approach, then use the term "direction", and speak in shorter time periods. This can narrow the focus and make it less overwhelming. If the purpose is not talked about, not relevant and not engaged with, then it is meaningless and worthless to our pursuit of rhythm. When referred to often, it is a performance asset.

4. **Utilise heritage.** What artefacts does your business have? Our past is a great inspiration to the future and reminds us what this place is all about. The Sam Antonio Spurs basketball franchise in the NBA is a great example. The team has an old giant rock hammer placed at the entrance of its home base. It also has a quote hanging on the walls (in five languages, so players and staff from around the world can understand it). It says:

    "When nothing seems to help, I go look at a stonecutter hammering away at his rock perhaps a hundred times without as much as a crack showing in it. Yet at the hundred and first blow it will split in two, and I know it was not that blow that did it, but all that had gone before." – Jacob Riis

This is part of the head coach's master plan to build purpose and unity in his team. Gregg Popovich is the longest-serving active coach in the NBA and major US pro sports leagues, with the most consistent record in the history of the league (talk about tenacity!). He has achieved five NBA titles, 22 Western Conference Division titles, has won more games as a coach than anyone else in the history of the league, and has a winning record for most consecutive seasons. A record that is beyond the best of the best. This is built on many mantras and philosophies, but a cornerstone is the use of heritage and the rock hammer to instil purpose into all players; to chip away and get 1% better every day. No matter the circumstances, if you are winning or losing, the complexity dissolves when all you need to worry about is getting 1% better today.

Defining a purpose and having a shared purpose for your team is a useful tool to leverage and keep people moving forward during tough situations. Purpose upholds motivation when the chips are down and builds continuity into your team amid changing staff, projects and team focuses. If purpose is cloudy or inconsistent, then people will be wondering why they should care or commit, and all sorts of friction will dominate your team's workflow.

2. Passion

Our emotions are powerful. If we do not feel anything for a task or goal, then it becomes meaningless, and we give up easily. We need to find *passion* for whatever it is we are tasked to achieve. I feel it is one of the most difficult things for many of us to generate in our modern lives. Not many people are doing their dream job, and if they are, there are still a lot of tasks within the job that are not fun, exciting or interesting. So, how do we remain passionate? Finding a mechanism to tap into and breed passion is not only useful but essential to building tenacity. As a leader, you need to feel passion for what you do and instil it in others.

Controlling and utilising passion to keep going and inspire others to keep going lifts team performance. Active and regular displays of passion are clear signals of intention, meaning, importance and desire. It is an effective way to gain positive responses in the people around you. When in line with focused goals and relevant problem solving, passion is a powerful way of sustaining high performance and making it contagious.

However, passion can also be the source of destructive team environments. Ryan Holiday states, *"Passion is the reason why people fail, not the reason why people succeed."* Holiday sees passion as the reason why we:

> *"Over-invest, under-invest, act before we are really ready, break things that require delicacy out of drunkenness of passion."*[71]

When passion is a form of unbridled enthusiasm with little thinking and strategy, it can set us up to do a lot of hard work with little result. We see people following their passion in business and end up in bankruptcy. We see people follow their passion in adventure (climbing mountains and exploring the Arctic), needlessly killing themselves and others. Heeding Holiday's warning may save us from the road to extinction. So, how can passion be helpful for leaders and team performance?

To benefit from passion as leaders, we need to show public displays of it. Our facial expressions, movements, tone of voice, tempo of movement and the look in our eye say a thousand words. This is powerful because, as humans, we have something called *mirror neurons* in our brains. Scientists at the University of Wisconsin published this finding in 2004 and described it as a phenomenon called *brain connectedness*. This is our need to mimic what we see operating below our consciousness. It explains why when we see someone smiling, we immediately smile as well, even though we may not know the person or know why they are smiling.[72] It is a type of contagion that happens between us, except it is not a viral infection – it is an emotional thought infection.

Also, we can benefit from a change in mindset via the use of body language. When we display our passion physically, we usually become more animated, enthusiastic and positive in our non-verbal language. Amy Cuddy is a social psychologist and author who has researched non-verbal communication deeply. Her research tells us that when we power pose, we can feel stronger and more confident. A change of our internal chemistry promotes alertness, focus and a lowered stress response.[73] [74]

Displaying passion not only invigorates us; it also energises others. Immediate motivational uplifts enhance engagement and flow, and contribute to people being in rhythm.

Ways to build passion and increase tenacity:

1. **Avoid harmful passion.** Impulsive, irrational, unbalanced and self-involved acts of passion rarely end with good team performance outcomes. This contributes to poor decision making and exclusivity. Knock harmful passion on the head – it creates a red mind instead of a blue one (humility – emotional control) and needless friction.

2. **Show enthusiasm.** When in a meeting, giving a presentation or saying "hi" in the morning, give it a little more enthusiasm than the bare minimum. If you are not enthusiastic, why should anyone else

be? But be sure to do it in your style and your way. For introverts or low-key people, you can show enthusiasm through eye contact, questions and one-on-one follow ups, to name a few examples. Whatever form it comes in, be sure to communicate your excitement in your facial expression, tone of voice and general demeanour. Rhythm is ongoing, and enthusiasm is a great tool for sustaining it, especially in a team environment.

3. **Set the tone.** In good times and bad, your team looks to you. The way you walk into a room, start a meeting and interact with clients shows others the way things should be done. Being intentional and even planning ahead will ensure you impact the behaviours of others around you. Subtle adjustments in posture, eye contact, tempo of stride and speech are all relevant. Once, I watched some politicians walking from their cars and entering a building for a cabinet meeting. I saw one state premier walking without a single thing in their hand. They didn't have a hair out of place and had a stride of zero waste. They were noticeably calm yet purposeful. Then, the next premier arrived, desperately grasping files, struggling with two heavy briefcases in one hand and trying not to spill their coffee in the other. They found it difficult to walk straight. I wondered which state parliamentary team was watching this and thinking that their boss was ready to represent and kick some butt? Which team would have felt slumped and defeated before a word was said? No matter the actual performance, your tone is a visible message to the team that either instils confidence or sucks it out of them.

4. **Recognition.** In the UK, an ex-staff member of mine moved on to work with Apple. When we caught up for a drink a few months later, she told me that in their work culture, everyone was required to recognise colleagues doing good work. This meant that if you saw someone do something well, you had to stop what you were doing, go to them and tell them. I find this a little creepy and possibly distracting in reality, but the principle is excellent – especially for leaders. Thank yous and well dones go a long way and can never be underestimated. With heartfelt emotion, it is a powerful use of passion.

5. **Focus.** If a leader gushes over anything and everything using broad strokes and meaningless buzzwords, their message can lose importance. Conversely, when we show passion in a direct, specific and considered way, it becomes exceptionally more powerful. For example, if a leader focuses on detail and accuracy as a priority principle for the team, and a report is delivered with these attributes, it is cause for passionate acknowledgement – even if the report missed the deadline. The leader's consistent show of passion removes doubt from the environment, upholding rhythm.

We do not need to generate a list of things we are passionate about in our work, even though this could be helpful. What we need to do is display our passion in ways that uplift our team. The improved confidence and will to succeed give everyone an emotional reason to push forward and tap into sources of tenacity they didn't realise they had. Our ability and that of our team to develop and sustain rhythm dramatically lifts.

3. Perseverance

At the heart of tenacity is the ability to *persevere*; to keep trying even when we are not succeeding. It sounds simple, but when we are failing, we tend to give up easily. Talent, socio-economic background, heritage, education and genes seem to fly out the window when the going gets tough.

When Angela Duckworth was trying to figure out what the number-one predictor of future success was, there were the obvious assumptions that it had something to do with talent, intelligence and environmental factors. These were all relevant but did not tell the true story. Duckworth, a professor of psychology at the University of Pennsylvania, decided to focus her research on this gap in our knowledge of performance.

Duckworth's premise was that it was those with *ferocious determination* and a clear and explicit direction who did the best. She formed a list of criteria to understand this better. *The grit scale* was born: a tool for understanding a person's level of grit. Subjects filled in a grit scale form before undergoing difficult projects. Duckworth's most famous study was of the cadets at the West Point Military Academy in the US. Every year, West Point receives 14,000 applicants. Once the physical and academic tests are done, only 1,200 gain admittance. Then, within the first two months, the Beast is responsible for an average of another 240 cadets to drop out. But what is the Beast?

The Beast is a gruelling 5am to 10pm schedule conducted seven days a week for seven consecutive weeks. No breaks and no contact with home are allowed. Described in the West Point handbook as *the most physically and emotionally demanding part of your four years at West Point,"* it breaks many a cadet every year. When Duckworth matched the grit scale with the number of cadets who remained after the Beast, the correlation was clear: those who dropped out had low grit levels. For two years running, Duckworth predicted – with better accuracy than any other metric – the cadets who would drop out during the Beast. The test was also conducted on people in sales – one of the toughest jobs in the professional world – with similar accuracy. High school graduates, Green Beret training and National Spelling Bee contestants were all part of the study, and all came back with the same results: perseverance and success are linked. And our ability to persevere is a major contributor to our tenacity levels.[75]

When we relate this to our workplaces, the opportunities are all around us. How many times have you seen new processes and initiatives put into place, only for them to be ditched a week or month later? When I reflect on this in my career, I see it has happened a lot. Almost systemically, this scenario repeats, causing workplaces to tread water and continually work hard for no progress. On an individual level, how many times have we given up on ourselves, and our manager has allowed us to do it? How many times have you let a team member give up? Persevering is an important learning curve and can be the catalyst for a lot of growth and betterment. If we can eradicate patterns of "giving up", our ability to reduce workloads and friction points is infinite.

Of all the ways to enhance tenacity, perseverance is the most tangible. It can be grown in a similar way to building strength and muscle mass in the gym. There are practices we can put in place to make perseverance an asset that allows us to perform at a higher level and lead others effectively for longer periods.

Duckworth speaks of many ways to increase our grit. Here are some exercises that relate to our leadership context for rhythm:

1. **Interest.** Relate a personal interest to the work you do. Finding a connection with your work gives you a meaningful reason to keep at it. For a family man who sells insurance, it may be something to do with his own accident history, where insurance helped his family through a hardship. A mechanic may have an interest in police forensic television shows, making every day at the workshop an opportunity to work through "cases" that must be solved. Whatever works for you and your personality. Write it down and use it in your daily language or post it somewhere so you can see it.

2. **Practise.** Malcolm Gladwell says we must do something for 10,000 hours to become an expert in our field. This speaks to repetition and experience over time. To maximise your time and focus, pick one thing to practise every day until you master it. Repetition is the road to excellence. It also teaches us to persevere through adversity, pain and frustration. I recommend going for something small (e.g. learning formulas on Excel or using a planning template before every meeting).

3. **Hope.** The ability to carve out positive self-talk that makes tomorrow look brighter than today. According to the Hay Group, this is called *realistic optimism* and is a key component of building resilience capability – a close bedfellow of perseverance. Not only is this important for leaders who are under tremendous strain and pressure, but it is even more important for leaders who want to keep their team in the game when things look or feel desperate. If there is no hope, we stop, and any form of flow, momentum and rhythm dies.

Perseverance is the steel inside us that allows the fluid and flexible body to do its magic in a dynamic and ever-changing environment.

4. **Playing fields.** Setting ourselves a playing field is another way of setting ourselves a challenge in a specific area to build a new or improved ability or discipline. The game is to pick one personal playing field and one professional playing field. They come with three rules. Firstly, everyone has at least one playing field. Secondly, the individual chooses their field. Lastly, you are allowed to give up! But only at a natural finishing point. For example, if you were to start learning the guitar, the natural stopping point would be at the end of the six-week online course you signed up for. If you were to learn how to build websites, then the stopping point could be the moment you finish creating your own website.

Perseverance takes a lot of work. But it's less work than if we give up often (or tolerate excuses from others regularly). We need to go through some difficult times and face our deficiencies when building our perseverance. It can be confronting, but trying to achieve anything of worth without perseverance is like being a professional criminal. You end up working harder to be a gangster than if you had just got a paid job. Perseverance is the steel inside us that allows the fluid and flexible body to do its magic in a dynamic and ever-changing environment.

The HAT competencies are a rich and deep area of opportunity for everyone. Each small area can be practised regularly, enabling any leader to make dramatic strides forward in the way they work and the amount of rhythm they bring to their work environment. The competencies take any performance base and make it better. They help us honestly assess our base and find the solutions to improve it. They also allow us to animate our base in our individual style. The HAT competencies represent a world of opportunity we can revisit at any point in our leader's journey.

The Leader's Constant

"We're going to battle and we're not expecting to come back alive or injury free, so let's throw everything at it."
– Inia Maxwell, Maori cultural expert, describing the Haka

When leading high-performing teams, we need to manage some *non-negotiables*. Another way of putting this is that if these critical things don't exist in a team, then more work for less return will be all but guaranteed. The pursuit of rhythm is not possible without cultivating and promoting three elements consistently. As we learnt previously, we are *experts in resistance* (see Chapter 1), and we will face a brutal onslaught of forces that want to diminish our ability to get into and maintain rhythm. It is for this reason leaders need to have the following three constants front of mind:

1. **Courage.** The ability to face scary things. We need the boldness to explore spaces that have not been experienced before and to do this wholeheartedly, without hesitation. From a team perspective, 99% in is not enough. Hesitation still exists. Garnering a mindset in your people that is 100% courageous is difficult, but it's imperative. Leaders must breed an environment where creativity, innovation and vulnerability are not only encouraged but a way of doing business. If we are courageous, we can hold the space for any conversation, no matter how awkward or difficult. And if we can do that, we can slash hours, days, months and even years of hard work from our workplaces.

2. **Confidence.** The absence of doubt, uncertainty and self-imposed limitations. When we are confident, we believe we can take on

challenges and know that no matter the outcome, we will come out the other side stronger, wiser and even more capable. We trust the systems, equipment, tools, capability, decisions and people in our teams and the wider company. There is a natural self-efficacy felt by everyone, which breeds the conviction that any challenge can be overcome. It is not arrogance; it is a trusting belief at the centre of synchronisation.

3. **Commitment.** A loyalty and respect for the people and community being represented. We need to feel a connection with our work and team that runs deeper than money, career progression or one's self-interests. A sense of belonging with cohesion between the players creates a tightness and affinity that's not only enjoyable for everyone but also attracts like-minded talent. It's the sort of environment where everyone is completely focused on contributing and problem solving without distraction during the toughest and most dire of situations. No one thinks about leaving or jumping ship. Buy-in is complete, meaning everyone is present and working in harmony. Full commitment removes the endless friction points many leaders deal with daily, which are costly, wearing and time consuming.

Courage Breeds Courage

When it comes to performance, what is it we need? From the previous chapters, we know we need to engage with the work at hand, gain flow within ourselves and repeat it. This is rhythm. But dynamic internal and external forces constantly challenge this, creating friction. Our pursuit of performance becomes jagged, sluggish and difficult. Sometimes, this friction expresses itself in the form of years of struggle without a sense of moving forward at all. So, we must be able to break free of these environmental constraints. We must shift our mindset from "fixed" to "growth", according to professor Carol Dweck.[76] We must make decisions in the moment, without hesitation to face the scary stuff, and know we will come out the other side stronger, wiser and with a positive outcome.

Easier said than done. But it is courage that allows us to do this. It is courage we need to promote in our people, for without it, they will live in a state of fear, hesitation and the misplaced belief that they are not good enough or empowered enough to change what must change. Courage is the first thing a leader needs to find within themselves and inspire in their people. The tools described in the humility and audacity sections in Chapter 6 are a path to increasing courage.

If we look at the brilliant work of Kim Scott, co-founder of Candor Inc., and her concept of *radical candour*, we will see a great model of what courage looks like from a communication point of view. As a long-term director at Google and then a faculty member at Apple University, Scott saw the very best and very worst of performance management. What Scott's experiences told her was that feedback could be destructive when it lacked "personal care" (humility) and did not "challenge directly" (audacity). Radical candour promotes what Scott calls *"a bullshit-free zone"*. It gives people a complete honesty that will make them better. It is private, respectful, immediate and helpful. I have found that being warm is also of huge benefit when delivering feedback of any nature. As a leader, we may find this confronting and scary. That is the point. These are the moments when we need to be courageous. We must remember that our feedback comes from the right place and is in service to the person we are speaking to.

When this type of communication becomes the norm, everyone in the team feels empowered and more comfortable to have these conversations with each other, their clients and even you! All of a sudden, there is mutual accountability and everyone's involvement and engagement in the problem-solving process increases.

Your team always looks to you and observes you to see how you act and approach challenges. If you show that you are willing to stand up to the board regarding cutbacks or that you are willing to ask the client that extra question to find out the real reason why they are delaying their investment, people take notice. When they see you come through the other side unharmed and with positive results, they have the courage to take a leap or have a go themselves.

Nelson Mandela famously said, *"I learned that courage was not the absence of fear, but the triumph over it. The brave man is not he who does not feel afraid, but he who conquers that fear."* Feeling the fear is good. It means we care and are stretching ourselves. As leaders, being comfortable with the uncomfortable is probably the first thing we need to learn about the gig. Using the humility and audacity competencies will fast track your ability to not only do this but also to turn it into a way of working. Once people in your team see it is safe to try new things, speak up, experiment and even make mistakes, they will feel free to be brilliant. More brilliant than they ever thought they could be. They will begin to breed courage amongst each other, their clients and maybe even you!

Never feel the effects of shrinking again. Never kick yourself for not piping up again. Never feverishly scramble to cover your tracks again. Why? Because you have been upfront, honest, open and transparent from the top, meaning ambiguity, delays and misalignments simply cannot exist. If they do, they are minor missteps rather than catastrophic falls. If we nurture a team environment where these frictions are regularly snuffed out, our ROE will continually increase.

Believing in Confidence

Jonathon Welch is an Australian choral conductor who established the Choir of Hard Knocks in 2006. It was an ambitious project created in conjunction with the Australian Broadcasting Corporation (ABC) for a television documentary. The premise was to make a platform for homeless people to come together and sing, and to see what effects it would have on them. Welch could never have imagined what would happen next. The choir became an ongoing group that performed on some of the biggest stages in the country. They had chart-topping albums and formed into an established charitable foundation that continues to inspire disadvantaged people around Australia.[77]

Another example of a choir creating hope and personal change for communities is the Song Keepers, an Aboriginal women's group from Central Australia. They have become a serious force musically and have even toured Germany![78] In both cases, marginalised people were brought together to sing, and everyone's lives dramatically changed for the better. They all became happier and healthier, and formed a stronger community. But how did getting a bunch of people together to sing make such a big change to their lives (and their communities)?

It comes down to the feeling of *worthiness*, as Dr Brené Brown calls it. Studies show there are many benefits to choir singing. From a physiological level, there is a synchronisation of heartbeats.[79] From this, there is a connectedness and an inclusiveness people respond to positively. There is a sense of belonging and safety, which had been missing from the lives of those in the choirs. Along with this, there is an opportunity for emotional expression, which positively changes people's brain chemistry and allows for improved mood and thought patterns.

Finally, the biggest surprise for everyone in the choirs was that they demonstrated to themselves they could achieve something they had previously thought impossible. This is critical. By coming together to perform, they increased their self-efficacy and, therefore, their resilience. They started to believe in themselves. That belief created a newfound confidence that cannot be underestimated when it comes to team performance.

Do we believe we can achieve what we want to achieve? Do we believe in our systems? Our structures? Our people? No matter what, a leader's job is to find and display this belief to promote an environment of belief. Welch used the platform of choir singing. Your platform is your business: the meetings, conversations, conferences, reports and phone calls.

By the way, the answer to confidence and belief is not to form a choir, even though that would be great, too! It is to use the audacity proficiencies to find new platforms and ways for people to express themselves. When this aligns with the tenacity proficiencies, we show ourselves that owning a task or project to the end is all it takes to achieve. By hook or by crook, the ability to "hang in there" is one of the best ways to gain belief and conviction.

Never feel the effects
of shrinking again.
Never kick yourself for
not piping up again.
Never feverishly
scramble to cover
your tracks again.
Why? Because you
have been upfront,
honest, open and
transparent from
the top.

From a confident position, we don't worry about whether something is possible. We concentrate only on how our tasks will be done and nothing else. We approach our work from a place of knowing it will be done rather than hoping. Rhythmic teams do not hope things will turn out well. They use hope and breed hope in those who do not have confidence because they know progress will be made no matter what.

The Commitment Model

The value of a leader having high levels of courage and confidence and building these attributes within their teams is clear. But if there is one thing anchoring these two ingredients, it is *commitment*. This ensures courage does not turn people into rogue agents or lead them to do things for their own benefit. Commitment also helps keep confidence from turning into arrogance, when a person wears the face of confidence, but there is no substance behind it. Leaders must drive commitment to ensure people feel a sense of belonging and cohesion. Then, an affinity is felt by all. I believe affinity is a critical achievement for any group, as it brings attention and desirability to a body of work that creates unstoppable momentum and increased performance with little effort (see attractors in Chapter 4).

When commitment is high, there is a stream of problems we do not need to worry about. We do not need to be overly polite or worry about hurting people's feelings, as they do not care for such pussy-footing – they just want the work they are involved in to be good. We don't need to worry about rousing people with big speeches because they are already highly engaged and gagging to get amongst it! And we never have to pander to people who think they are too talented or indispensable, as they will happily fall in line so they can showcase their expertise and look good anyway as part of a champion team. Commitment not only feels great (one of the best bits of leading with rhythm!); once again, it removes doubt, distraction and hesitation. To be "all in" is a liberating space to be in. We can completely let go of exterior needs, allowing our attention to focus solely on the work at hand.

We know all of this occurs in teams due to the Stanford Project, which we discussed in Chapter 3. This taught us that of all the models used to set up a team, the Commitment Model worked the best across multiple metrics. Michael Beer, director of TruePoint Partners management consultancy and author of *High Commitment, High Performance*, has researched companies that base their culture on commitment. He calls them *high-commitment, high-performance management firms* (HCHP), where there is an alignment between the people, as well as between goals, structures and measures. Their psychology is aligned in terms of purpose, meaning, impact and overall expectations.[80] Other than the social competencies, the analytical 5xM Framework (Chapter 4) is the tool all leaders can use to get these things clear and aligned.

In a high-commitment team, the capacity for learning and moving through change is aligned so that ego cannot exist, and open, honest collective thinking drives transformation. Beer has found this model of working is the most valuable in pulling an organisation out of a crisis, and creates long-term resiliency in a business so it can ride out the tough times and consolidate in the good times (i.e. rhythm). Beer uses Southwest Airlines, Johnson & Johnson and Hewlett-Packard as examples of long-term HCHP companies that have successfully navigated six decades using commitment as their cultural compass. Beer also names companies where new CEOs used the HCHP framework to pull the organisations out of crisis. Beer's examples include General Electric, Campbell's® Soup, IBM and the British supermarket chain Asda. It is evident that the Commitment Model is a concept worth investing in as a leader.

Commitment works. Top-down autocratic dictation does not inspire people to engage and step wholeheartedly into the project at hand. When commitment is experienced and felt, momentum builds. A tightness forms and the collective safety and cohesion make synchronisation so much easier to obtain. If you have ever seen a high-board diver commit fully to a dive and hit the water sweetly, compare that diver to one who hesitates. You will see the obvious difference. It is an extreme visualisation of the concept; a dive may only take a few seconds, while we may work with a team to create progress over years.

Yet, just as a hesitant diver can unravel mid-air, so, too, can our teams unravel mid-day, mid-week, mid-year or mid-project. The result can be catastrophic. The high costs of recruiting and retraining team members while missing deadline after deadline hurt businesses significantly. The cost of stress levels can cause traumas that last for years, as well as commercial costs that not only hit share prices and future budgets but also reputations and trust in the brand's capability to deliver.

When a leader openly shows they are in it for the client, the business, the community and the staff, it is a vote for commitment. When a leader matches this with the desire to hang in there no matter what, people mirror this and feel compelled to hop in the trenches to the bitter end. All this forms a solid base of commitment from which everything else can grow.

A devastatingly potent combination of all-in desire (commitment), spark and flair to create (courage), and freedom to be brilliant (confidence) makes for an unstoppable team – a team that is in flow more often than not. The ability to help each other get into and maintain flow has been built. It is an environment where people collectively rinse and repeat this flow state to the point where rhythm is ongoing, and they are in a situation of high capability. Alignment and clarity soar, coupled with an emotional capacity to serve, lead and grow. It is a never-ending cycle that allows ordinary people to come together to achieve things they had never believed possible.

Inspiration – How Leaders Leverage Courage, Confidence and Commitment

Working in the beauty industry opens your eyes to an interesting world of art mixed with health, science and commercial business. I was a naturopath who had a performance background in sport and an operational management grounding in retail and wholesale. I had exposure to small business, national-sized business and global corporate business. I had worked direct to consumer (B2C) and business to business (B2B). It has been a unique journey, but by far the most captivating world I worked in was the salon industry. Trying to find the commercial connections between art, marketing, trends and communities was like trying to solve a Rubik's Cube (which I have never been able to solve). Clients could be highly demanding (especially in the luxury end of the market, which I operated in). Hairdressers could be temperamental – they saw themselves as artists, meaning anything to do with commerciality was a slight on their professional standing. Conversely, corporate management could be brutal in their expectations of business departments and results – no matter what!

As an outsider, I found myself forming a management style that understood the human side of business. It did not come easily to me, as I swayed from being perceived as a forceful, abrupt tyrant to a soft touch and pushover. Sometimes, it felt like I swung from one to the other on an hourly basis, depending on who I was dealing with.

But most fascinating was the high importance put on inspiration for collections and brand launches. Hairdressers bought into this deeply. It became the platform for robust and highly charged discussions, at the pub and in the conference room. Collection launches and events were some of the best parties I had ever been to. Catwalk shows, launch parties, national conferences and global gatherings were all brilliantly good fun. But when the champagne stopped flowing and the hangovers dissipated, inspiration was what everyone constantly spoke about as being connected with business results. I always found it hard to buy into and a bit of a stretch to say that inspiration was related to business performance.

After the best part of a decade in the industry, without even noticing it, I finally got it. It hit me in the face in a heated boardroom meeting of national managers. The national education manager was presenting their plans for the next six months, which would be the basis for motivating and upskilling the hairdresser network in our client salons. This would be the foundation for driving product and salon consumable sales. On this day, the national education manager was talking about the need to focus on selling. He then said something I never thought a senior hairdressing manager would say: *"Inspiration never put money in the till."*

I remember it as if it happened five minutes ago. I was astounded. What astounded me more was my reaction. As a person who was always commercially minded in this world of beauty, I found myself arguing with the "artists" in the room. After years of witnessing inspiration as the central theme of a business model, I was now starting to understand it. I took umbrage to the idea that inspiration did not matter all. And I take umbrage to it to this day. Inspiration is one of the most important (if not the most important) things we can provide. It is the vehicle by which everything else is delivered. If people are not inspired, why would they care? Why would they engage? Why would they serve, question or hang in there during the tough times? Everyone needs inspiration.

To inspire is essential when it comes to leadership. Inspiring others to be better, care more and take action is the most fundamental principle we can utilise when aiming to further ourselves and our projects. The reason for this is inspiration links directly to our hearts (or our emotions). It is our emotions that rule our decision making and govern our direction. We like to think we are rational creatures, but we are not.[81] How else can you explain why a person would complain about poor customer service wasting their time, when the complaint itself takes more time to lodge than the initial incident? I have been on the receiving end of such complaints and have lodged them myself as a customer. It happens all the time because we are highly emotive beings.[82]

Douglas Van Praet, author of *Unconscious Branding: How Neuroscience Can Empower (and Inspire) Marketing*,[83] says it well:

> *"The most startling truth is we don't even think our way to logical solutions. We feel our way to reason. Emotions are the substrate, the base layer of neural circuitry underpinning even rational deliberation. Emotions don't hinder decisions. They constitute the foundation on which they're made!"*

It is for this reason that we must inspire our people every single day. Inspiration comes before motivation, job experience and job knowledge. Without inspiration, people don't have the drive to bring their skills and expertise alive. We must inspire and reach people's hearts with every message we send. But what messages do we need to send? What is it that will enhance performance and create a rhythm people can own and perpetuate?

As leaders, we have a choice to inspire our people with a world full of concepts, ideas and philosophies. If rhythm and ultimate synchronisation between our people and community are what we want, then it is clear what we need to display to inspire those around us:

Courage, confidence and commitment.

We will use the social proficiencies to do this on a daily basis:

Humility, audacity and tenacity.

We will use the analytical and technical proficiencies to create constructive feedback and ongoing execution:

The universal leadership toolbox, the unique technical audit and the 5xM Framework.

As leaders, we will use these pillars to build our unique language and leadership style to suit our personality and situation. We can build momentum as we work through our leadership journey from survivor, to existor, to follower, to motivator, to attractor and all the way to progressor. Towards the top of this journey, we turn initial momentum into acceleration and forecastable performance, as we are able to maintain steady, resilient performance no matter what external or internal frictions we experience. And we will ward off factors of resistance that want to push us back into states of extinction and isolation. We will maintain a strong, durable culture of consolidation and synchronisation. All by being the inspired leader and inspiring those around us. If we do this, there is one guarantee: it will be rewarding, enjoyable and there will certainly be money in the till!

Mastering Rhythm

"Talent is only the starting point."
– Irving Berlin

Experiments Eat Actions for Breakfast

The marshmallow challenge teaches us many things, but the ultimate lesson is that problem solving is best done by kids. It turns out that adults need to learn from kindergarten children. For those who have never experienced the marshmallow challenge (spoiler alert!), it is a facilitation game where a group is divided into teams of four or five people. Each group is given the same resources: a yard of string, a yard of tape, 20 lengths of uncooked spaghetti, one standard-sized marshmallow, and 18 minutes. Each team needs to build a self-standing structure on a tabletop to hold the marshmallow as high as possible. The team that builds a self-supporting structure with the highest marshmallow wins.[84]

It is fun, it is frantic, and it quickly gives us insights into what "good" looks like in terms of team performance and leadership. Originally developed by Peter Skillman, Tom Wujec made the exercise popular when he used the challenge as part of his work as a technology pioneer.[85] He found that kindergarten children, on average, performed better than many other groups, including CEOs and business school graduates. After collating a lot of data, Wujec and his team discovered that professionals tended to have a similar way of working, which harmed their results.

Professionals seemed to follow a distinct process with four distinct phases. Firstly, they would *orient*. This involved figuring out a hierarchy, how they would tackle the problem and brainstorming. Then they would *plan*: who would do what and how they would put their ideas together. Next was the *build* phase. Finally, they would *deliver*, which Wujec and his consultants called the "ta-da moment" – the reveal of their final work. The problem was that the ta-da moment often became an "uh-oh moment", where the untested final structure would buckle or not turn out as hoped.

Children took a different approach. They played. They didn't have a meeting to figure out who was in charge – they just picked things up and started playing with them. They tested a lot, failed fast and kept working on things that didn't fail. This meant no time was wasted, and a lot of options were experimented with before a final product was produced. We need to acknowledge that some groups of children ended up in a mess, but so did a lot of the adults! I once ran this exercise with a group of executives, where one team used so much time discussing irrelevant details, they didn't even realise they had tape until there were two minutes to go. They ended up producing a structure that held the marshmallow just two inches off the table (the worldwide average is approximately 20 inches).

As professionals, we have a lot to lose. We are taught to manage risks or be risk averse to maintain safety. So, we plan and take tentative steps towards new things. This has its merits, but it also has its limits. Finding safe and risk-acceptable ways to experiment is a clear and productive way to move things forward practically while accelerating learning. This last point is critical for leaders wanting to understand rhythm as a concept to increase performance and create an environment of synchronisation. However, I do not believe we experiment well in our modern organisations, and my experience in learning and development is a great example of this.

As an educator who has run hundreds of training days, I have used action plans in almost every session I have run. The premise is that a person has sat in a room learning for a few hours or a day. It is then time for the learner to agree on and commit to what they will do next to create change. This makes perfect sense, except for one problem: people don't always act on the back of the learnings. And if they do take action, they typically try something once or twice, and if it does not work out, they consider it a failure and revert to their old ways of doing things. It is a frustration of every stakeholder in the process, and a fundamental reason why management training alone is not an effective way to embed learning and change.

The *Learn Apply Reflect Model* has proven to be the most reliable model for learning, according to a survey by McKinsey & Company in 2012. It found that approximately 10% of training is retained. Up to 70%-80% of learning becomes embedded in professional leaders when new skills are applied in real workplace scenarios. And the final 10%-20% of learning comes from reflecting on and sharing thoughts and experiences.[86] [87] This model helps us understand the importance of coaching and ongoing peer discussion. It also shows us the limits of taking learnings and turning them into a mere checklist of actions – especially if people cross these actions off their list as "done" when the result was poor (which is often the case when trying something for the first time). In some cases, it can put great pressure on the learner, who is aware that a lot of investment goes into training days, and *performance increases* are expected. Also, don't forget about the poor consultants. Our reputations are on the line!

Approaching our learnings with the spirit of play and experimentation is much more productive. Experimentation and play do not mean there is no accountability or the learning is in any way less serious. On the contrary, experiments require data, adjustments and rigour, and are only entered into with the intention of them being successful. Play is also a serious business. It is a way of working to achieve results, as the worldwide facilitation phenomenon called LEGO® *Serious Play* shows us.[88] This is a facilitation system that helps business teams solve problems. Play is a way to improve through *doing* while being *relentlessly curious*. The marshmallow challenge is a microcosm of business that shows us the power of play to achieve better results quickly. The explosion of agile as a framework for project teams all over the world, especially in tech, speaks to this idea also.

We can lead a culture where people continually practise a range of disciplines they can call upon at will, like an archer who reaches for an arrow. Through this practise, these disciplines form into a sequence of habits that magically happen.

Any leader can turn learnings from the Rhythm Effect principles into new ways of leading their team in a short period. Experiments turn into conclusions, as assumptions are quashed, and the learnings are leveraged into tangible, ongoing business results. Make action points and take action, but remember that the "doing" is in the application and iteration of the principles to suit your personality, style and unique challenges. Collect data, have regular discussions with peers and a mentor, and constantly update. It may take a dose of audacity to do this and break with current conventions, and possibly even some imaginary rules! I call this "walking through the door".

Practise is the Discipline

The hardest thing about my work with leaders is getting them to walk through the door. When I deliver a coaching program or lead a workshop, I often get buy-in and knowing nods – the look people give you as they look into your eyes, nodding to say they are with you and totally get what you are talking about. People acknowledge the principles and intellectually understand them. When we discuss scenarios and the relevant tools to use, everyone takes their notes and off they go. Sometimes, when I talk with them a few weeks later, I find out they have implemented very little. This is when the excuses flow:

- *"Oh, it's been so busy! I haven't had a chance to use anything yet."*
- *"I haven't spent much time with my team, so there hasn't been a need for any of this leadership stuff."*
- *"It's been hard to find the time to do any of the stuff we talked about."*

It is ironic. The work we have discussed is designed to help with all of the above and can be applied to any workplace scenario. This experience tells me that many of us cannot "walk through the door" into the new paradigm, even though it is open nice and wide, with an encouraging usher waving people through. We emotionally hold onto what we have been told all our lives: *"If in doubt, work harder."* The dramas we have become accustomed to may cause us all sorts of pain, but letting go of them is like saying goodbye to a dear friend forever. But the main reason why leaders find it hard to experiment is that it is new. It is scary. There is the great unknown of what will happen, and our fight/flight/freeze lizard brain kicks in and thinks of every possible worst-case scenario. Courage, confidence and commitment are not at the levels required.

So, we keep doing what we were doing before.

How can we break this cycle? If we do not undertake learning and development, we will experience friction throughout our entire careers. If we continue to invest in learning and development but with little change in behaviour, then we will turn the whole process into a tick-box exercise with little benefit to stakeholders. It leaves us with one option: we need to focus our energy on becoming expert *walkers through doors*.

The ability to practise is what we must demand of ourselves. It is the underlying skill all other things are built on. This is why we are told to practise at home every day between guitar lessons. Why a cricketer bowls a ball 100 times at training two or three times a week between games. Why a comedian rehearses their set over and over again until the timing is spot on.

As mentioned in Chapter 6, Malcolm Gladwell made the 10,000 hours principle famous with his book, *Outliers: The Story of Success*.[89] The idea is that practising something for 10,000 hours makes you an expert. It's a nice, general principle that, even if not entirely correct, tells us that repetition gives us a set of experiences that are important if you want to be good at a particular skill or profession. A more pointed reference to this idea is Josh Kaufman's *The Personal MBA*, where he proposes that it takes 20 hours of practise to go from *"knowing nothing to being pretty good"*.[90] [91] This means you could take one concept from this book and practise it for 45 minutes every day for a month to achieve a "good to expert level" of building rhythm into your workflow and team. Winning!

Whatever system you prescribe to, it is clear the one pathway open to all of us is practise. To do the doing over and over. It is the one way we get better at anything, particularly if it is *deliberate practise*. Originally coined by psychologist K. Anders Ericsson,[92] this is when we engage in a type of practise that is systematic and purposeful so that we can learn a specific skill. When deliberate practise is supported with structured mentoring or coaching, a mechanism is set up to ensure feedback, accountability and execution take place without exception.[93] Experiments have a distinct timeline and are purposeful, with direction and a finish line in mind.

When we hear the word *discipline*, many people immediately think of the military or a strict parent. One of my favourite internet memes says, *"Discipline is what you do when no one is looking."* But in our context of leading rhythm, practise becomes a discipline. It is a skill or attribute. Formed from the Latin word disciplina, meaning *"instruction, knowledge"*, discipline relates directly to being a learner. With this construct, we can make learning through practise a skill that we carry with us throughout our careers. It can be applied to every job and workplace. I find this idea to be extremely helpful when trying to understand what behaviours we are recruiting for and what we want to see in our team cultures for better performance.

If we are good learners through practise, then we can learn and excel at pretty much anything. Adding deliberate practise to our repertoire of skills means we are not only able to walk through the door to new paradigms more easily, but we can also run through multiple doors rapidly. We perceive "failures" as fun little moments of learning. The adjustments become easier, our ability to be vulnerable elevates and our need to be perfect all the time diminishes. As Thomas Edison said, *"I have not failed. I've just found 10,000 ways that won't work."*

As leaders, not only is practise the way to grow and amplify your Rhythm Effect, it is also an important skill to role model and thus create an environment of learning, growth and excellence. I find it to be an exciting proposition as an educator and supporter of all the good, hard-working people out there striving to be their best and make a difference in their workplaces and communities. The ability to turn learning into a series of experiments that are practised non-stop as a way of working is critical to finding rhythm.

Autonomy Turns Skills into Mastery

When someone learns a new language, they begin with little understanding and speak with a "broken tongue". Then, they develop some form of semi-fluency and graduate to being fluent. What is the difference between someone tripping over every second word and someone who understands not only every word but also the nuances in the sentence structures and enunciations? They have made the skill a part of them, with a deep knowledge that they can apply in a multitude of circumstances. No longer do they have to consciously think about the next word or the meaning they want to convey. The language just happens.

In our workplaces, I feel this is exactly what we are aiming to achieve when developing our leadership skills and team performance capabilities – *autonomy*. The ability to execute in autopilot without hesitation or need for conscious thought is liberating and supports elite outcomes. Aside to this is the lack of need for help from others. We do not need to defer to others for guidance or insight. This is exactly where we want to be as leaders and, crucially, how we need our team members to operate.

Using the rhythm building blocks to identify the key skills and traits we want to see in all our people consistently is the first step. Then we can practise these disciplines to the point where we are confident, committed and courageous in using them every day until they become automatic. Everyone is then able to operate with a solid level of autonomy and express themselves through their work, freeing up hundreds of hours across the team over the course of a year. This is the path to mastery.

The pathway from learning to mastery is to build good habits and break bad ones. James Clear, international authority on habits, gives us an updated version of this topic utilising the work of predecessors such as Charles Duhigg and B.F. Skinner. Some fundamentals Clear speaks about in his book, *Atomic Habits*, include understanding the compounding effect of habits, the relationship between habits and identity, and the four elements of a habit: a cue, a craving, a response and a reward. When we zoom out from the all-consuming day-to-day tasks, we can understand our larger goal: to set up a sequence of habits to form the way we work. By doing this, we can see our path to becoming excellent at what we do. As leaders, if we promote an environment where people can build their skills into habits to the point of mastery, we have the bones of a system that will gain momentum through sheer acceleration (i.e. rhythm).

I am a firm believer this is the future of leadership and community progression. An ability for everyday people to define important skills, align their behaviours with their mission, and maximise their daily interactions. We can lead a culture where people continually practise a range of disciplines they can call upon at will, like an archer who reaches for an arrow. Through this practise, these disciplines form into a sequence of habits that magically happen.

The final destination of mastery is only possible when autonomous decision making takes place without hesitation or deferral. If this was to occur in your workplace, how many headaches and mistakes would be avoided? How many personality clashes would simply not happen? And how many more people would want to join your party?

It is an exciting prospect for any high achiever. It is a wonderful opp-ortunity to spawn a unique culture that suits your personality and that of your people and organisation. But what do you do once mastery has been achieved, and the results of synchronisation have been experienced repeatedly? The achievement may, in a sense, become boring.

Mihaly Csikszentmihalyi, world-leading authority on *flow*, names the stages that occur when we fall out of flow. This is when a person's skill level is out of balance with the challenges they face. Maybe things have become a little too easy. In this case, the first stage was to go from being in *flow* to being in *control* – a state that is comfortable but not overly exciting. Then, if left unchecked, we can fall into a state of *relaxation*, which is even more comfortable but with little psychological engagement. And if there is further deterioration, where skills start to slip and the level of challenge or responsibility lowers, a state of *apathy* sets in – a typical trait of an existor in the leader's journey. It would be such a shame to slip back into apathy when mastery was possible.

It is for this reason that relaxation and boredom are signposts that tell us we have mastered what we are doing. A professional who becomes brilliant within their role is a great example. They have achieved repeated success and it is all starting to come a little too easily. It is enjoyable and a nice feeling, but when high achievers experience success for too long, things start to slip. The person has achieved rhythm in their workflow and it is time to look at the next challenge. The building blocks of rhythm need to be approached at a higher level. This may mean a salesperson begins to take responsibility for key accounts, or a team member steps up into a supervisor's role. The cycle starts again with a new set of defined rhythm building blocks.

In a team context, a version of the *Tuckman Model* may be experienced. The journey towards synchronisation may feel like going through the stages of forming, storming, norming, performing and eventual adjourning, where a team dismantles and starts again.[94] We see this in sport, when the most successful teams dismantle aging squads and rebuild with the next generation. As a leader, being able to zoom out and see this game is of great value. It reduces the fear of losing good people to the very progress you have helped create. There is an opportunity to be a part of other people's story, but not to dominate it. There is an opportunity to part company with them on good terms, wish them well and continue to be in each other's network, where you may once again help each other in the future. It is a liberating way of working and is embedded in the ideals of the Rhythm Effect.

When we see the world through this lens and operate as an agent of rhythm, there is no losing. Nelson Mandela once said, *"I never lose. I either win or learn."* This sums up the spirit of the ROE game; a point of view where energy is not lost on the things out of one's control and where we are not obsessed with our scoreboard. To freely and openly admit we are not all born progressors, and we have a long journey towards becoming a leader who operates with deep, consistent trust.

It is freeing, dissipates tension and focuses on the truly important things: our interactions. The hundreds and hundreds of opportunities we experience every day. Moments we can make the most of, learn from and frame constructively and helpfully.

To engage with rhythm, explore it and integrate it into one's way of working is an achievement of itself. But to keep rhythm to one's self would be selfish. Being a leader of impact, where ripples are felt long and wide, even after you have moved on, would really be something. It is a worthy pursuit to spread and share with as many people as possible. I have experienced this in my day-to-day work, and it brings me more joy than anything else. Seeing others increase their capability and getting those shots of happy hormones, which only come with ongoing flow and the feeling of true achievement, is infinitely rewarding. I want this for you and everyone you work with.

The aim of the game is to achieve without burning company resources, bridges or ourselves. The default of hard work does not cut it for you or your team. Synchronisation is the pinnacle of excellence and what a leader can focus on to create performance, mastery and even legacy.

Infinite possibilities are out there waiting for us all. The door is open. Let's walk through it and bring our people along for the ride.

The Body of Work Continues

The entire system of rhythm is broad and full of endless learning. It may even be overwhelming. Where do you start?

As an executive coach, management mentor, facilitator and speaker, it is my job to add even more depth and understanding to the principles outlined in this book. Helping leaders decipher and diagnose their points of rhythm is how I spend my waking hours. My recommendation is to start small. Always start small. Pick one concept in the book you feel most confident about utilising. The biggest mistake many people make is to try to transform entire business cultures after reading a book such as this. Full marks for enthusiasm, but it will not yield rhythm.

Some options for further insights and support can be found in the following places:

1. **Resources.** Ready to read, download, consume and use. Visit www.paulfarina.com.au/resources to enjoy a range of rhythm-building assets to become the best leader you can be.

2. **The Boot Room.** A community of like-minded leaders and high achievers interested in understanding and increasing rhythm in their work lives. You will receive my latest insights and research, as well as "community only" content the general public cannot access. Free and available to any professional with an internet connection and an email address! Visit www.paulfarina.com.au.

3. **Speaking.** A large area of my work is speaking about the principles of rhythm at conferences, industry events, dinners and expos. Conducted in the flesh or online, I enjoy sharing the stories

and research I have collated and curated, which help people move from the friction-filled old paradigm towards the new paradigm of rhythm. It is a wonderful opportunity to motivate and inspire new thinking and a new language. Visit www.paulfarina. com.au and contact me to discuss your next event.

4.   **Learning.** I love working one on one with leaders in my coaching and mentoring programs. With diagnostics, online learning modules and a raft of learning tools and supporting materials, these programs are designed for deep learning, experimentation, building practise and creating autonomy. These high-impact programs are true accelerators. Other options include team training and facilitation programs to deep dive into specific elements of the Rhythm Effect to target the outcomes and goals an organisation requires. Consumed as micro sessions or as an entire suite, these programs are brilliant for bringing people together on a journey of learning.

5.   **Cultural Shift.** A combination of all the above to create cultural programs. Tailored and comprehensive in nature, this is an opportunity to use the principles of the Rhythm Effect so they can emanate through entire teams, departments and organisations, creating elite synchronisation.

Having read *The Rhythm Effect: The Leader's Guide to Team Performance*, you are now an agent of rhythm. Observe it in the conversations and work environments you step into. Once you have a clear understanding of the principles, you will start to see it everywhere. This awareness serves us well so that we may create impact and reduce friction – for ourselves and, more importantly, for others.

This is what leaders do. Play well!

References

1. Brown, Brené. (2012). *Daring Greatly: How the Courage to Be Vulnerable Transforms the Way We Live, Love, Parent, and Lead.* New York: Gotham Books.

2. "Workplace Stress Continues to Mount." Korn Ferry. https://www.kornferry.com/insights/articles/workplace-stress-motivation

3. "Two thirds of business leaders have suffered from mental health conditions." Bupa. (2018). https://www.bupa.com/newsroom/news/business-leaders-mental-health-study

4. "Workplace Stress Continues to Mount." Korn Ferry. https://www.kornferry.com/insights/articles/workplace-stress-motivation

5. "Sunday Scaries." The Sleep Judge. (2019). https://www.thesleepjudge.com/sunday-scaries/

6. Kravitz, D. A., & Martin, B. (1986). "Ringelmann rediscovered: The original article." *Journal of Personality and Social Psychology.* 50(5), 936–941. https://doi.org/10.1037/0022-3514.50.5.936

7. Afshar, V. (2018). "New Research Uncovers Big Shifts in Customer Expectations and Trust." Salesforce. https://www.salesforce.com/blog/2018/06/digital-customers-research.html

8. Nandkishore, N., and Lafferty, J.M. (2018). "Going extinct: why corporate giants die." Think at London Business School. https://www.london.edu/think/going-extinct-why-corporate-giants-die

9. Roach, D. (2016). "These 5 beer makers own more than 50% of the world's beer." Business Insider Australia. https://www.businessinsider.com.au/biggest-beer-companies-in-the-world-2016-1?r=US&IR=T

10. Belludi, N. (2008). "Albert Mehrabian's 7-38-55 Rule of Personal Communication." Right Attitudes. https://www.rightattitudes.com/2008/10/04/7-38-55-rule-personal-communication/

11. Pash, C. (2018). "Australian's job churn has taken a turn for the worse." Business Insider Australia. https://www.businessinsider.com.au/australian-jobs-turnover-churn-robert-half-2018-6

12. Heffernan, M. (2015). *Beyond Measure: The Big Impact of Small Changes.* Simon & Schuster.

13. Parks, C.D., and Stone, A.B. (2010). "The desire to expel unselfish members from the group." *Journal of Personality and Social Psychology.* 99(2), 303-310. https://psycnet.apa.org/record/2010-14719-007

14. Howard, T. (2019). "McLaughlin reveals title decider panic in new book." Speed Café. https://www.speedcafe.com/2019/02/28/mclaughlin-reveals-title-decider-panic-in-new-book/

15. Poynter, R. (2020). "Customer Complaints and the Silent Majority." Potentiate. https://www.potentiate.com/Latest-Insights/Customer-Complaints-and-the-Silent-Majority/Latest-Insight-Details

16. Pash, C. (2019). "Foxtel revenue is falling but subscriptions surge through its new streaming services." AdNews. https://www.adnews.com.au/news/foxtel-revenue-is-falling-but-subscriptions-surge-through-its-new-streaming-services

17. "Redefining business success in a changing world: CEO Survey." 19th Annual Global CEO Survey. PricewaterhouseCoopers. (2016). https://www.pwc.com/gx/en/ceo-survey/2016/landing-page/pwc-19th-annual-global-ceo-survey.pdf

18. Drane, R. (2015). "How Gennadi Touretski Revolutionised Swimming Training." Inside Sport. https://www.insidesport.com.au/news/how-gennadi-touretski-revolutionised-swimming-training-422661

19. Wathen, A. (2017). "The Olympic Preparation of Alexander Popov by Gennadi Touretski (1996)." American Swimming Coaches Association. https://swimmingcoach.org/the-olympic-preparation-of-alexander-popov-by-gennadi-touretski-1996/

20. Carey, A. (2020). "Inside Australia's 2020 retail bloodbath as brands rocked by mass closures by mid-January." News.com.au. https://www.news.com.au/finance/business/retail/inside-australias-2020-retail-bloodbath-as-brands-rocked-by-mass-closures-by-midjanuary/news-story/14c50866e94b06b94f2a392310a12056?utm_medium=Facebook&utm_campaign=EditorialSF&utm_content=SocialFlow&utm_source=News.com.au

21. Kelly, M. (2013). "Poor concentration: Poverty reduces brainpower needed for navigating other areas of life." Princeton University. https://www.princeton.edu/news/2013/08/29/poor-concentration-poverty-reduces-brainpower-needed-navigating-other-areas-life

22. Baron, J.N., and Hannan, M.T. (2002). "Organizational Blueprints for Success in High-Tech Start-Ups: Lessons from the Stanford Project on Emerging Companies." *California Management Review*. Vol. 44, No. 3. https://cmr.berkeley.edu/assets/documents/sample-articles/2002_44_3_4776.pdf

23. Ruiz, M. (2001). *The Four Agreements: A Practical Guide to Personal Freedom*. Amber-Allen Publishing

24. Brown, J.S. (2000). *The Social Life of Information*. Harvard Business Press.

25. Thomke, S. (2012). "Mumbai's Models of Service Excellence." Harvard Business Review. https://hbr.org/2012/11/mumbais-models-of-service-excellence

26. Pearce, E., Launay, J., and Dunbar, R.I.M. (2015). "The ice-breaker effect: singing mediates fast social bonding." The Royal Society Publishing. https://royalsocietypublishing.org/doi/full/10.1098/rsos.150221

27. Clift, S., and Morrison, I. (2011). "Group singing fosters mental health and wellbeing: Findings from the East Kent 'singing for health' network project." *Mental Health and Social Inclusion*. Vol. 15 No. 2, pp. 88-97. https://www.researchgate.net/publication/241675796_Group_singing_fosters_mental_health_and_wellbeing_Findings_from_the_East_Kent_singing_for_health_network_project

28. Klein, C. (2018). "Winston Churchill's World War Disaster." History. https://www.history.com/news/winston-churchills-world-war-disaster

29. Puiu, T. (2020). "Your smartphone is millions of times more powerful than the Apollo 11 guidance computers." ZME Science. https://www.zmescience.com/science/news-science/smartphone-power-compared-to-apollo-432/

30. Lusinski, N. (2018). "12 ways your smartphone is making your life worse." Business Insider Australia. https://www.businessinsider.com.au/12-ways-your-smartphone-is-making-your-life-worse-2018-6?r=US&IR=T

31. Newman, S. (2017). *The Book of No: 365 Ways to Say It and Mean It and Stop People-Pleasing Forever.* Turner.

32. Parks, C.D., and Stone, A.B. (2010). "The desire to expel unselfish members from the group." National Library of Medicine. https://pubmed.ncbi.nlm.nih.gov/20658845/

33. Kong, D.T., Konczak, L.J., and Bottom, W.P. (2015). "Team Performance as a Joint Function of Team Member Satisfaction and Agreeableness." Sage Journals. https://journals.sagepub.com/doi/abs/10.1177/1046496414567684

34. Kelley, R. (1988). "In Praise of Followers." Harvard Business Review. https://hbr.org/1988/11/in-praise-of-followers

35. "Gallup Q12® Meta-Analysis Report." Gallup. (2016). https://news.gallup.com/reports/191489/q12-meta-analysis-report-2016.aspx

36. Collins, J. (2001). *Good to Great: Why Some Companies Make the Leap... and Others Don't.* William Collins.

37. Pink, D.H. (2009). *Drive: The Surprising Truth About What Motivates Us.* Riverhead Books.

38. Sheen, T. (2015). "Jurgen Klopp believes Liverpool can 'win the title' in the next four years and describes himself as the 'Normal One'." *Independent.* https://www.independent.co.uk/sport/football/premier-league/jurgen-klopp-believes-liverpool-will-win-the-title-in-the-next-four-years-and-describes-himself-as-a6687446.html

39. Brand, G. "Jurgen Klopp's 10 Steps to Greatness." Sky Sports. https://www.skysports.com/football/story-telling/11669/11909299/klopps-10-steps-to-greatness

40. "Premier League Club Netspend for the last 5 Seasons." Transfer League. https://www.transferleague.co.uk/premier-league-last-five-seasons/transfer-league-tables/premier-league-table-last-five-seasons

41. Lane, B. (2019). "Liverpool FC is about to sign a Nike kit deal worth more than $91 million, the biggest in Premier League history." Business Insider Australia. https://www.businessinsider.com.au/liverpool-fc-to-sign-record-breaking-kit-deal-with-nike-2019-8?r=US&IR=T

42. Pearce, J. (2020). "'Jurgen surprises me every day. His brain works differently to other people' – Exclusive interview with Klopp's No 2 Pep Lijnders." The Athletic. https://theathletic.com/1513365/2020/01/08/liverpool-klopp-lijnders-interview/?source=fbpcadsbc&ad_id=23844049661710092&fbclid=IwAR2j-g0Nxa9BH3chQW3U4zfXQXuw1AfAmdPddnfo0EtdW7D1-BkInCMPw3A

43. Herbert, I. (2017). "Liverpool coach reveals Jürgen Klopp's methods and says he is '30% tactics, 70% team building.'" *Independent*. https://www.independent.co.uk/sport/football/premier-league/liverpool-news-jurgen-klopp-coach-reveals-methods-tactics-team-building-epl-a7529936.html

44. Kelly, R. (2020). "Premier League 2020 winter break: Why is it happening, FA Cup replay clashes & changes explained." Goal. https://www.goal.com/en-au/news/premier-league-2020-winter-break-changes-explained/18rrncxdnwxc21mn6eaxnu4j5y#:~:text=The%202019%2D20%20Premier%20League,played%20on%20Saturday%2C%20February%2015.

45. Biss, M. (2017). "How to Improve Your Rhythm and Timing." Musical U. https://www.musical-u.com/learn/how-to-improve-your-rhythm-and-timing/#

46. Stoller, J.K., Goodall, A., and Baker, A. (2016). "Why The Best Hospitals Are Managed by Doctors." Harvard Business Review. https://hbr.org/2016/12/why-the-best-hospitals-are-managed-by-doctors

47. Davis, C. (2018). "Japan steal World Cup hearts with dignified response to cruel exit." *The Telegraph*. https://www.telegraph.co.uk/world-cup/2018/07/03/japan-steal-world-cup-hearts-dignified-response-cruel-exit/

48. Torio, L., and Ghani, F. (2018). "Gracious in defeat, Japan leave Russia World Cup with pride." Aljazeera. https://www.aljazeera.com/news/2018/07/gracious-defeat-japan-leave-russia-world-cup-pride-180703091649322.html

49. Dickson, J. (2011). *Humilitas: A Lost Key to Life, Love, and Leadership*. Zondervan.

50. Smith, J. (2015). "17 Billionaires Who Started Out Dirt Poor." Inc. https://www.inc.com/business-insider/billionaires-who-went-from-rags-to-riches.html

51. Sinek, S. (2013). *Leaders Eat Last: Why Some Teams Pull Together and Others Don't*. Portfolio.

52. Albeck-Ripka, L., Tarabay, J., and Kwai, I. (2020). "As Fires Rage, Australia Sees Its Leader as Missing in Action." *New York Times*. https://www.nytimes.com/2020/01/04/world/australia/fires-scott-morrison.html

53. Werner, J., and Lyons, S. (2020). "The size of Australia's bushfire crisis captured in five big numbers." ABC News. https://www.abc.net.au/news/science/2020-03-05/bushfire-crisis-five-big-numbers/12007716#:~:text=More%20than%2012.6%20million%20hectares%20burned&text=According%20to%20the%20Department%20of,the%20NSW%20Rural%20Fire%20Service.

54. Coyle, D. (2018). *The Culture Code: The Secrets of Highly Successful Groups*. Random House.

55. Kerr, J. (2015). *Legacy: What the All Blacks Can Teach Us About the Business of Life*. Little, Brown Book Group

56. *Sunderland 'Til I Die*. (2018). Netflix.

57. Deutschman, A. (2009). *Walk the Walk: The #1 Rule for Real Leaders*. Portfolio.

58. "Nordstrom Company History." Nordstrom. https://www.nordstrom.com/browse/about/company-history

59. Sinclair, N. (2017). "Why Nordstrom is beating all of its department store competitors." Yahoo! Finance. https://au.finance.yahoo.com/news/nordstrom-beating-department-store-competitors-125704786.html

60. Linderman, M. (2010). "Nordstrom's Employee Handbook — short and sweet." Signal v. Noise. https://signalvnoise.com/posts/2632-nordstroms-employee-handbook-mdash-short-and-sweet#comments

61. Morieux, Y. "How too many rules at work keep you from getting things done." TED. https://www.ted.com/talks/yves_morieux_how_too_many_rules_at_work_keep_you_from_getting_things_done/transcript?language=en

62. Meyer, D. (2006). *Setting the Table: The Transforming Power of Hospitality in Business*. Harper.

63. "Research". Gregory M. Walton. gregorywalton-stanford.weebly.com/research.html

64. "History of the Royal Society." The Royal Society. royalsociety.org/about-us/history/

65. Useem, J. (2007). "Apple: America's best retailer." Fortune. https://archive.fortune.com/magazines/fortune/fortune_archive/2007/03/19/8402321/index.htm

66. Itzler, J. (2015). *Living With a SEAL*. Center Street.

67. Hutt, S., Gardener, M., Kamentz, D., Duckworth, A.L., and D'Mello, S.K. (2018) "Prospectively predicting 4-year college graduation from student applications." Proceedings of the 8th International Conference on Learning Analytics and Knowledge (LAK '18). Association for Computing Machinery, New York, USA. 280–289. https://doi.org/10.1145/3170358.3170395

68. Mourkogiannis, N. (2006). *Purpose: The Starting Point of Great Companies*. St Martin's Press.

69. Kets de Vries, M.F.R. (2019). "Is Your Corporate Culture Cultish?" Harvard Business Review. https://hbr.org/2019/05/is-your-corporate-culture-cultish

70. Clear, J. (2018). *Atomic Habits: An Easy & Proven Way to Build Good Habits & Break Bad Ones*. Avery.

71. Holiday, R. (2016). *Ego is the Enemy*. Portfolio.

72. Williams, J.H., Whiten, A., Suddendorf, T., and Perrett, D.I. (2001). "Imitation, mirror neurons and autism." *Neuroscience & Biobehavioral Reviews*. https://pubmed.ncbi.nlm.nih.gov/11445135/

73. Carney, D. R., Cuddy, A. J. C., and Yap, A. J. (2010). "Power Posing: Brief Nonverbal Displays Affect Neuroendocrine Levels and Risk Tolerance." *Psychological Science*. 21(10), 1363–1368. https://doi.org/10.1177/0956797610383437

74. Cuddy, A.J.C., Schultz, S.J., and Fosse, N.E. (2018). "P-Curving a More Comprehensive Body of Research on Postural Feedback Reveals Clear Evidential Value for Power-Posing Effects: Reply to Simmons and Simonsohn (2017)." *Psychological Science*. https://doi.org/10.1177/0956797617746749

75. Duckworth, A. (2016). *Grit: The Power of Passion and Perseverance*. Collins.

76. Dweck, C. (2006). *Mindset: The New Psychology of Success.* Random House.

77. Hull, D. (2007). "Choir Offers Sanctuary from 'Hard Knocks'." Encore Magazine.

78. Chalmers, M., Attard, M., and Brierley Newton, L. (2018). "How an Aboriginal women's choir ended up in Germany, singing Lutheran church songs in the languages of Australia's Central Desert." ABC News. https://www.abc.net.au/news/2018-04-19/lutheran-songs-in-the-language-of-the-central-desert/9672498

79. Dingle, G. A., Brander, C., Ballantyne, J., and Baker, F. A. (2013). "'To be heard': The social and mental health benefits of choir singing for disadvantaged adults." *Psychology of Music.* 41(4), 405–421. https://doi.org/10.1177/0305735611430081

80. Lagace, M. (2009). "High Commitment, High Performance Management." Harvard Business School. https://hbswk.hbs.edu/item/high-commitment-high-performance-management

81. "The Dangerous Myth of the Rational B2B Buyer." DeSantis Breindel. (2015). https://www.desantisbreindel.com/insights/emotional-b2b-buyer/

82. Baum, D. (2017). "How Emotion Influences Buying Behavior (And Marketers Can Use it)." iMPACT. https://www.impactbnd.com/blog/emotion-influence-buying-behavior

83. Van Praet, D. (2012). *Unconscious Branding: How Neuroscience Can Empower (and Inspire) Marketing.* St. Martin's Press.

84. Anthony, S.D. (2014). "Innovation Leadership Lessons from the Marshmallow Challenge." Harvard Business Review. https://hbr.org/2014/12/innovation-leadership-lessons-from-the-marshmallow-challenge

85. Wujec, T. (2010). "Build a tower, build a team." TED. https://www.ted.com/talks/tom_wujec_build_a_tower_build_a_team?language=en

86. Levy, A. (2018). "Why Leadership Training Doesn't Work." Forbes. https://www.forbes.com/sites/forbescoachescouncil/2018/02/23/why-leadership-training-doesnt-work/#2ca2762d77a4

87. Gurdjian, P., Halbeisen, T., and Lane, K. (2014). "Why leadership-development programs fail." McKinsey. https://www.mckinsey.com/featured-insights/leadership/why-leadership-development-programs-fail#

88. LEGO® Serious Play. https://www.lego.com/en-us/seriousplay

89. Gladwell, M. (2008). *Outliers: The Story of Success.* Little, Brown and Company.

90. Kaufman, J. (2010). *The Personal MBA: Master the Art of Business.* Portfolio.

91. Long, J. (2016). "The Importance Of Practice – And Our Reluctance To Do It." Harvard Business Publishing. https://www.harvardbusiness.org/the-importance-of-practice-and-our-reluctance-to-do-it/

92. Clear, J. "Deliberate Practice: What It Is and How to Use It." James Clear. https://jamesclear.com/deliberate-practice-theory#:~:text=Deliberate%20practice%20refers%20to%20a,specific%20goal%20of%20improving%20performance.

93. Phillips, J.J. (1996). "ROI: The search for best practices." *Training & Development.* Vol. 50, no. 2.

94. "Forming, Storming, Norming, and Performing." Mind Tools. https://www.mindtools.com/pages/article/newLDR_86.htm

Glossary

5xM Framework – the master model for the analytical proficiencies. When the five Ms are in sync and understood clearly by a leader, they can align team members with processes proficiently to fuel rhythm.

7-38-55% rule – Albert Mehrabian's concept concerning communication. It states that humans receive messages in three different ways: spoken words contribute 7% of a message, tone of voice contributes 38%, and body language contributes 55%. It is not so much a rule but more a helpful communication principle, and generally only relates to Western societies.

Agile – a method of project management used especially for software development, characterised by the division of tasks into short phases of work and frequent reassessment and adaptation of plans.

Analytical proficiencies – critical thinking skills that enable a leader to constantly discuss, question and eventually align the overarching mission with the daily moments and every stage in between.

Attractor – a leader with a reputation and ongoing leadership style based on respect, which culminates in the marketplace and workforce advocating their work and/or product.

Audacity – an act of courage or confidence that other people find shocking or disrupting. A leadership skill utilised to inspire innovation and belief.

Autocratic model – a team based on the premise of monetary motivations, control and coordination through close personal oversight, where employees are selected to perform pre-specified tasks.

Autonomy – the ability to make your own decisions without being controlled by or deferring to anyone else.

Belonging cues – verbal and non-verbal signals that create safe connections in the workplace and are critical in ensuring active participation and inclusion.

Bureaucratic model – a team based on challenging work and/or development opportunities and formalised control, where individuals are selected based on their qualifications for a particular role.

Business lifespan – the period for which an organisation is expected to work properly or last.

Commitment Model – a team based on emotional and familial ties of employees to the organisation, where people are selected based on cultural fit.

Consolidation phase – when a team or business invests in learning, development or experimentation, which improves Return On Effort (ROE) but is often accompanied by lowered or lagging performance results.

Crunch time – when the pressure to succeed is great, often towards the end of an undertaking.

Culture of service – where service to external and internal customers is prioritised in all goals, decisions, actions and everyday operations. An emotional and shared connection to service is a part of how everyone works.

Don't get its – people who do not understand that their work is a place of opportunity for improvement, betterment, learning and problem solving.

Engineering model – a team based on attachment through challenging work and peer group control, where people are selected based on specific task abilities.

Expert leaders – leaders with a comprehensive understanding of the technical skills of people under their remit of responsibility.

Extinction phase – when a team or business operates without viability, where high levels of resources are being used to obtain a low level of return. A short-termism mentality and culture are associated with this phase of the ROE scale.

Existor leaders – leaders who work in an agreeable manner so that they do not create more work for themselves. They are happy to maintain the status quo as long as it does not adversely affect themselves or their interests.

Fast fashion – inexpensive clothing produced rapidly by mass-market retailers in response to the latest trends.

Finite mindset – the perspective that rules, goals and outcomes in our business or team are fixed, agreed and locked in. It is a mindset that inhibits adaptability, does not entertain the possibilities within constraints, and does not understand the fact we are playing a game that never ends.

Focus of appeal – the single most compelling reason why one would buy your product/service, speaking to a specific audience's need while also doing this better than any other competitor. A marketing concept used to define marketing messages.

Followers – leaders who keenly listen to and follow the instructions of predecessors, dominant competitors or senior mentors. They tend to be reliable in nature and results but are restricted in their influence on performance due to their lack of experience, critical thinking or agility in dealing with challenges and friction points without external help.

Friction – any process, person, tool, routine, way of thinking, communication technique, pattern of behaviour, model of working or interaction that is dysfunctional to the point of creating more or unnecessary work, or more monetary, time or human cost than the bare essential.

Game of ROE (Return on Effort) – a scale that measures a leader's progress not only in performance results but also in the use of rhythm to gain performance that is both sustainable and resource efficient.

Get its – people who understand that their work is a place of opportunity for improvement, betterment, learning and problem solving. Often referred to as high achievers.

Grit scale – devised by Angela Duckworth and her research team as a set of measures designed to measure trait-level perseverance and passion for long-term goals.

Groupthink – a psychological phenomenon that occurs within a group of people whose desire for harmony or conformity in the group results in an irrational or dysfunctional decision-making outcome.

HAT competencies – an acronym of the set of skills that come together to make up the social proficiencies of rhythm: *humility*, *audacity* and *tenacity*.

High-commitment, high-performance management firms (HCHP) – organisations that balance the somewhat opposing characteristics of *performance alignment, psychological alignment* and *capacity for learning and change*. Advocated by Michael Beer (Professor of Business Administration, Harvard Business School).

Horizontal business model – where points of the business supply chain are not owned by one company. In the context of this book, it is where a company manufactures their product, and then sells it on for others to distribute either wholesale or retail.

Humility – putting the needs of another person before your own and thinking of others before yourself. A leadership skill utilised to inspire commitment and psychological safety.

Isolation phase – when a team or business achieves acceptable levels of performance via isolated elements of best practice, or with strain to near breaking point on isolated areas of the operation. It is associated with a lot of very hard work without consistency or risk-diversification.

Key performance indicator (KPI) – a measurable value that demonstrates how effectively a company, department, team or individual is achieving key business objectives.

Leader's journey – describing the stages of development a leader takes to become the most influential agent of rhythm to achieve meaningful, ongoing progress.

Learn Apply Reflect Model – a proposed model of how professionals upskill from education programs. It states that 10% of learning comes from the training experience itself, 70%–80% comes from applying the newly learnt skills on the job, and the remainder 10%–20% comes from sharing and reflecting upon those experiences.

Level 5 leaders – a concept developed in Jim Collins' book, *Good to Great*. Level 5 leaders display a powerful mixture of personal humility and indomitable will. They're incredibly ambitious, but their ambition is first and foremost for the cause, for the organisation and its purpose, not themselves.

Mastery – comprehensive and expert knowledge of a skill, subject or field.

Mission – the ultimate reason for an entity's existence. The paramount effect a person, team or organisation is trying to achieve through its plans or actions.

Moments – the daily interactions and behaviours people enact with their peers, customers and stakeholders.

Motivation – derived from the word "motive", which means the needs, desires, wants or drives of an individual. It is the process of stimulating oneself or others to act to accomplish goals.

Motivator leaders – leaders who are engaged in the problem-solving process of their business. They are engaged in their people's plights and journeys and are engaging themselves. Motivators spend high volumes of time discussing and mentoring others to generate elevated levels of care, attention and loyalty to the projects they lead.

New paradigm – utilising alternative ways of working to the traditional means of working harder, working longer and spending more on resources to solve problems or correct inaccuracies/inadequacies. An updated method using communication, mindset and implementation techniques/models/tools to remove friction points and avoidable tensions that are unproductive or destructive.

Old paradigm – the traditional means of solving problems in the workplace, where people work longer, harder and/or require higher levels of resources. A method of working that values high inputs rather than efficient inputs.

Performance base – the consequence of the technical proficiencies and analytical proficiencies. When technical and analytical skill levels are high, the result is a capable and clear-minded leader and team.

Performance execution – the consequence of the social proficiencies and the technical proficiencies. When social and technical skill levels are high, the result is consistent and elite-level output.

Performance feedback – the consequence of the analytical proficiencies and social proficiencies. When analytical and social skill levels are high, the result is effective and swift communication, adjustments and/or learning.

Power pose – using expansive body poses to trigger feelings of increased strength and power. Also called postural feedback.

Progressor leaders – leaders who are deeply trusted by their community while able to generate deep trust in themselves and the people they work with. Not only are they able to achieve deep trust, but they also provide the cultural and environmental factors for a team to create significant positive change and equitable progress for all stakeholders.

Protectionist mindset – a need or want to keep what one has achieved or acquired to oneself rather than collaborating, sharing or co-creating with others for the benefit of the whole. It is often driven by fear, ego and selfishness.

Purpose – the reason for doing or creating something. A reason why an initiative exists.

Radical candour – to care personally for another person and humbly share with them your opinions while directly challenging their behaviour, decisions or work. It is confronting while being kind, respectful and warm in nature and delivery.

Realistic optimism – using factual evidence of achievement to build a positive or optimistic mindset of what one can achieve. The focus on past successes instead of past failures helps increase a person's resilience and, therefore, their ability to face future challenges due to increased belief and a lowered burden of failure.

Return on Effort (ROE) – the performance one achieves for the efforts exerted.

Rhythm – a strong, well-defined and regular pattern of movement that is ongoing, fluid and synchronised.

Servant leadership – first coined by Robert K. Greenleaf in the 1970s, it describes a leader who bases their reason for being a leader on their service to others rather than to accumulate and increase their own power. The servant leader primarily focuses on the growth and wellbeing of the people and communities they belong to.

Shared economy – an economic model defined as a peer-to-peer (P2P) based activity of acquiring, providing or sharing access to goods and services. It is often facilitated by a community-based online platform.

Skills audit – the process of listing the skills requirements of a role, team or organisation and critiquing the level of competence to understand where improvements can be made and which areas should be prioritised.

Social loafing – the phenomenon of a person exerting less effort to achieve a goal when they work in a group. It is regarded as one of the main reasons why groups are sometimes less productive than the combined performance of members working as individuals.

Social proficiencies – the self-management and relationship-management skills that enable a leader to make high-quality decisions, communications and actions that promote high-performing environments with rhythm.

Star Model – a team based on challenging work, reliance on autonomy and professional control, where elite personnel are selected based on long-term potential.

Sunday dread – the anxieties one experiences on Sunday when thinking about the coming work week, school week or other obligations that await in the week ahead.

Survivor leaders – leaders who are fully focused on keeping their job, team or project alive and are, therefore, in a predominant state of flight/fright/freeze. They tend to operate in a perpetual cycle of short-termism where problems are solved transactionally, often resulting in damaged relationships, reputations, future opportunities and lowered influence. High levels of friction are experienced by default, and very high amounts of resources are spent for meagre outcomes.

Synchronisation – the coordination of events to operate a system in unison. Systems that work with all parts in synchrony are said to be synchronous or in sync and are associated with rhythmic people, teams and organisations.

Synchronisation phase – when a team or business operates in harmony with very few jagged friction points and wasted resources. A calm and trusting mentality is prevalent, and cultural identity is consistent and strong throughout. This phase is at the very top end of the ROE scale, enabling infinite growth and possibilities.

Technical proficiencies – the skills a leader needs to execute their work to an elite level, including technical skills unique to the company, industry or expert field, as well as the management skills any leader must have to lead a team or project.

The Rhythm Effect – the outcomes and amplification of performance and positive change that result from an individual or team of people creating and operating in rhythm.

Tuckman Model – originally published by Dr Bruce Tuckman in 1965, this model describes a team's stages of development. It is now used widely as a template for understanding the development and maturing of a team throughout the following stages: forming, storming, norming, performing and adjourning.

Unique technical skills – the technical proficiencies one must aim to perform at an elite level to lead a team with rhythm. They are skills unique to one's position, company, industry and/or location.

Universal technical skills – the shared technical proficiencies every leader needs to perform at an elite level and lead a team with rhythm no matter what position, company, industry and/or location one operates within.

Vertical business model – where the end-to-end points of a business supply chain are owned and operated by one company. In the context of this book, it is where a company manufactures its product and distributes, wholesales and retails to the end consumer.

Walking through the door – knowing what needs to be done and why, and the consequences of doing or not doing that leadership action, and then doing it in a planned, conscientious and considered manner. The act of "doing it" is described as "walking through the door", and is often the most difficult thing a leader is required to do when implementing any concept in *The Rhythm Effect*.

Acknowledgements

Not only is writing a book a gigantic undertaking, but it is also part of a larger body of work full of learning, sharing, delivering and endless consultation. Many have invested time and energy into this journey with me, which has been as traumatic as it has been transformative! A big thank you to everyone engaged in the process, which has been defining for me from a professional and personal perspective. I am excited, as this book represents one step in a larger adventure, but I would like to acknowledge a few stand-out contributions.

Firstly, a shout out to the clients big and small, the associations and peak bodies, and the community networks that have invested in my programs and concepts. Our experiences together have helped shape and develop *The Rhythm Effect* to be as relevant as it has been vigorously examined in real time by the marketplace.

In the collation of the content, thank you to the endless list of people I interviewed in my pursuit of leadership, team performance and business theory to deepen my understanding of classic and contemporary principles. A special mention to key influences Daniel Coyle, Sam Walker, Angela Duckworth and Steven Pressfield.

There have been mentors along the way who have provided the platform and given guidance to shape this framework, including Bryan Whitefield, Rohan Dredge, Christina Guidotti and Stephen Scott Johnson. Thank you for your expert insights and generosity.

I have found myself relying heavily on several contemporaries for feedback, accountability and rich discussion to continually develop value in the marketplace, including David White, Mark Greaney, Shane Michael Hatton, Keegan Luiters and Clark Mitchell. I am a fan of all your works and thank you for your thoughtfulness, cleverness, friendship and humour.

My leadership has been heavily influenced by a wide variety of fantastic leaders I have had the pleasure of working with. A big thank you to some of the best in the business across industry, including Andrew Zesers, David McConnachie, Graham Clarke and Mette Haxthausen.

The publishing of this book has come together with a team of amazing professionals. Firstly, the trusted proofreading team of Sol Goodall, Tony McDonald, Dean Wallace, Simon Turner and David Polkinghorne – your feedback and insights enriched the book no end. The great work of designer extraordinaire Jansen Lye yielded results beyond expectation. For making me look as good as humanly possible, thank you to Fi Mims Photography. Lauren Shay from Full Stop Writing, Editing and Design has been a safe pair of hands for the cover design, copy-editing, typesetting and all-round amazingness. Sylvie Blair and the BookPOD team have been a guiding hand in the publishing and distribution of the book.

A big thank you to my assistant, Seiji Hojilla, for your tireless work and devotion to my entire practice. I could not have achieved what I have in my work without your consistent and caring input every step of the way.

Lastly and most impactful is the loving and unwavering support of my wife, Jana. You are my rock, chief challenger and cheerleader. We all need someone to believe in us, and your deep belief in me and what I can achieve has fuelled me more than you will ever understand. For this, I am grateful beyond words and deeply in love with the journey we are on together.

Thank you.